DIMENSIONS OF WAR

Understanding War as a
Complex Adaptive System

"Diplomacy and Strategy"
English Series
Directors: Fouad Nohra and Michael J. Strauss

Diplomacy and Strategy is a collection initiated by the academic directorate of the Centre d'Etudes Diplomatiques et Stratégiques to promote the outstanding scientific work presented by Ph.D. graduates, professors and researchers. The scope of subjects covered is as wide as international relations itself, encompassing disciplines such as political science, economic science, international law and sociology.

OTHER TITLES

DUQUESNE Isabelle, *Nepal, Zone of Peace. A Revised Concept for the Constitution*, 2011.

STRAUSS Michael J., *The Viability of Territorial Leases in Resolving International Sovereignty Disputes*, 2010.

Diplomacy and Strategy Series

Samuel Solvit

DIMENSIONS OF WAR

Understanding War as a
Complex Adaptive System

By the Same Author:

RDC : Rêve ou illusion ? (Editions L'Harmattan)

© L'Harmattan, 2012
5-7, rue de l'École-Polytechnique ; 75005 Paris

http://www.librairieharmattan.com
diffusion.harmattan@wanadoo.fr
harmattan1@wanadoo.fr

ISBN : 978-2-296-99721-9

EAN : 9782296997219

To Géraldine

TABLE OF CONTENTS

Acknowledgments 11

Preface 13

Introduction 17

PART I. THE SIMPLIFICATION AND REDUCTION OF
WAR CONCEPTUALIZATION 23

Chapter 1. Classic Conceptions of War 25
   Toward Peace: Hobbes, Kant and Montesquieu 26
      Hobbes 26
      Kant..28
      Montesquieu..31
   War as a Tool: Machiavelli and Clausewitz..........................33
      Machiavelli 33
      Clausewitz...34
   The Use of Conflict Through the Perspective of Historical
   Materialism: Lenin's Wars and Revolutions........................37

Chapter 2. Contemporary Perspectives 41
   The International System Induces War: The Neo-Realism of
   Kenneth Waltz...41
   War Is What States Make of It: The Constructivist
   Perspective 43
   War and Economics 45
   War as a Destructive Phenomenon: Peace Research and
   Conflict Resolution Studies...48

PART II. A GENERATIVE SOCIAL PHENOMENON,
UNCERTAIN AND SELF-MODIFYING 55

Introduction 57

Chapter 3. The Dimensions of War 59
   A Space-Time Construct 59
   A Social Process..61

Chapter 4. A Productive Phenomenon 69
   Uncertain, Autonomous, and Self-Modifying 70
      Unpredictable 70
      Autonomous and Self-Modifying 75
   War and Politics: A Dialectical Approach 80

Chapter 5. Understanding War as a Complex Adaptive
System 87
   The Notion of Complexity 87
   Complex Adaptive System 88

PART III. THE SECOND CONGO WAR AND THE US-
VIETNAM WAR 93

Introduction 95

Chapter 6. The Second Congo War (1998-2003) 97
   Actors' Trajectories and Interactions 98
   War System 102
      Economy Throughout War 102
      War Complex 105

Chapter 7. The US-Vietnam War (1954-1973) 109
   The Morass of Vietnam 110
   A Domestic Fight 114
   Reasons for War: From the Origins to the End 117

Conclusion 121

Bibliography 127
   Congo 143
   Vietnam 147

Abbreviations 149

ACKNOWLEDGMENTS

I would like to thank Professor Richard Beardsworth for his advice. His incisiveness and insightful comments were essential in helping me to clarify and theorize my reflection.

I am grateful to my friend Amos Schupak, who kept pushing me further during our discussions, and also to Richard Sheard, for being a patient listener during our weekly runs. I am thankful to Diane Schmitlin for helping me review this work, to Louis Gautier for having accepted to write the preface and for his comments, and to my editor, Michael J. Strauss.

Finally, this work would not have been possible without those who give me the energy to fight for a better world: Géraldine, Luca, Valérie, Antoine, Clara, Jacqueline, Valère, and Philippe.

And many thanks to all those who inspired me, helped me, and supported my work.

PREFACE

It is in Ithaca that I write this preface. In places of this sort it is impossible not to let one's thoughts be invaded by reminiscences of the Odyssey, that poem of deception that follows the Iliad in the Homeric cycle, the poem of force. Force, deception – regardless of the period, these are the bywords that govern war. The superiority of means and the intelligence necessary to surprise an enemy or to thwart its intentions have always constituted the rational foundations of military victory. Yet these human, too human, laws are also confronted on the battlefields with the uncertainty principle, the hand of the devil that can suddenly disrupt the most soundly established plans. Examples abound throughout history of the best armies being brought to disaster by fortuitous accidents, unforeseen circumstances, impulsive outbursts in the midst of strategic calculations.

This is what is well understood by Samuel Solvit, who is doubtless informed by his personal experience in Afghanistan, when at the heart of his work, *Dimensions of War*, he judiciously asserts: "War is uncertain or unpredictable because it is a nonlinear phenomenon... By definition, war is uncertain and theories are attempts to face this uncertainty. On the one hand, people and their theories try to master and forecast war, and on the other hand war is done because the future is not defined."

Having recognized that war is an "elusive" concept and that war theories account for this in ways that are imperfect, Samuel Solvit argues that we should understand war as a "Complex Adaptive System." To him, war resembles an ecosystem. Like a living organism, it is continuously being regenerated by internal factors and transformed through interactions with its environment. This demonstration is carried out in three steps: a critical analysis of the principal theories of war, an elaboration of the concept of the "Complex Adaptive

System" (CAS), and a pair of case studies that illustrate his thesis, the Vietnam War and the Second Congo War.

No matter how one may try to confine war within a bag of principles, it always escapes through a hole in the canvas. It is useless to pretend that we can understand war completely, even if classical theories may help to shed a useful light on it. One of the great merits of Samuel Solvit's book is, indeed, that he reviews these theories concisely and with clarity. To summarize Machiavelli, Hobbes, Kant, Montesquieu, Clausewitz, Marx, Waltz, Wendt... in about thirty pages is a feat! One cannot, therefore, reproach the author for leaving out others, like Hannah Arendt, or for abbreviating and streamlining the presentations of the many theses that are included. What counts is his conclusion, which I share, according to which any theoretical approach to war, whether it is meant for circumventing it intellectually or managing it in practice, oversimplifies what it really is.

Yet as attractive as Samuel Solvit's invitation may be, comprehending armed conflicts, notably contemporary ones, from the notion of CAS – that is to say, in a purely phenomenological manner – introduces other paradoxes in his argument. The empirical description of war certainly restores all of its complexity and shades, but the lessons learned are only of interest retrospectively. They cannot, moreover, be easily extrapolated from one conflict to another, and when this is done it is at the risk of improper generalization. The notion of CAS thus results in war being a "case by case" phenomenon, with the principal inconvenience of isolating their events and rendering impossible a philosophical/historical reading of what they nonetheless possess in common. For there is indeed an underlying unity and a continuity between phenomena as varied as a tribal raid, a Hoplite battle, combats among knights of the Middle Ages, a campaign led by Marshal de Saxe, the Napoleonic wars, the two World Wars, and the interventions in Libya, Iraq, and Afghanistan in this beginning of the 21st century.

In a way, the cases discussed in the third part of the work, the two episodes that entered world military history as the conflicts of Vietnam (1954-1973) and of the Congo (1998-

2003), affirm both the interest in analyzing these events as CAS (especially with regard to the study on the Congo war, the more singular of the two) and the risk that this type of analysis can make them historically "watertight."

Here and there, throughout his remarks, Samuel Solvit discreetly includes, as a counterpoint to his arguments, some more personal remarks derived from his own experience. They are always welcome, very pertinent and would sometimes deserve being developed more fully. But without a doubt, Samuel, somewhat more than Ulysses, was aware of the danger of being diverted and pressed on to reach safe harbor. This is what he succeeds in doing in this lively and constantly stimulating essay.

Louis Gautier
Ithaca, June 24, 2012

– Professor of Political Science, Université Paris I Panthéon-Sorbonne; Special Adviser for Defense to the French Prime Minister, 1997-2002

INTRODUCTION

*Presumptuous, deem'd, vain mortal! that his power
Should rise above the gods, and Neptune's might.
And was riot this the phrensy of the soul?*[1]

– Aeschylus

Think, too, of the great part that is played by the unpredictable in war: think of it now, before you are actually committed to war. The longer a war lasts, the more things tend to depend on accident. Neither you nor we can see into them; we have to abide their outcome in the dark.[2]

– Thucydides

In short, disorder saves the day – it guarantees our next breath regardless of where we happen to stand.[3]

– Neil Johnson

In modern world affairs, different forms of warfare are emerging that break previous categorizations of war and confuse our points of reference. Old categories used to assist in grasping "reality," but current realities do not seem to fit these designations any more. What was previously called "war" is contestable. Civil war, world war, total war, limited war, low-

---

[1] Aeschylus, "The Persians," in *The Plays of Aeschylus*, 472 BC, trans. Robert Potter, 4th ed. (London: George Routledge and Sons, 1895).
[2] Thucydides, *The History of the Peloponnesian War*, trans. Rex Warner (London: Penguin Books, 1972), 81-82.
[3] Neil Johnson, *Simply Complexity: A Clear Guide to Complexity Theory* (Oxford: Oneworld, 2007), 32.

intensity war, rebellion, guerilla, wildcat war,[4] molecular civil war,[5] intractable conflicts, neo-Hobbesian war,[6] banditism, terrorism, cold war, genocide, and a "failed state" situation are among the names found by recent academics and policy-makers to frame new hybrid situations. Indeed, classification is hard because conflicts are constantly changing in terms of actors, aim, context, means, place, and purpose.

Herfried Münkler gives an insightful description in stating that the course of new wars "is determined by the dispersion, not the concentration, of forces in space and time," and therefore "war becomes a way of life." Wars fluctuate between private and public, economics and politics, non-political and political, ideology and emotions, civil and international. Beyond the possible novelty of these wars, these categorizations avoid, voluntarily or not, focusing on war as a multi-dimensional phenomenon. These approaches remain descriptive, whereas war is productive by essence. It is similar to an unlimited run, because each war is different. There are as many categories of war as there are wars. So, in this period of mutable identities and various kinds of warfare, how do we further our understanding of what war is?

War should be conceptualized as a generative social phenomenon which is accordingly uncertain and self-modifying – in other words, it is a *complex adaptive system* (CAS). War is not a fixed event that can be understood as a mere instrument, it is rather a period and a space where groups experience processes of construction and deconstruction of themselves, their environment, and their relationships. By discussing the social, temporal, and spatial dimensions of war, this work exposes its unpredictability, complexity, change, and

---

[4] Herfried Münkler, *The New Wars* (Cambridge: Polity Press, 2005), 24. This term was initially developed by Wolfgang Sofsky "to reflect the re-emergence of marauding bands, the increasing frequency of massacres and the systematic use of rape as a war measure."
[5] *Ibid.*, 24. This term was initially developed by Hans Magnus Enzensberger to describe the mutations of civil wars in terms of actors and place.
[6] *Ibid.*, 24. Trutz von Trotha used this term to describe contemporary forms of small wars.

generativeness. War comes to resemble an "ecosystem," given that central to the ecosystem concept is the idea that living organisms are continually engaged in a set of relationships with every other element constituting the environment in which they exist.

Part I will review some of the most influential theories concerning war since Machiavelli – Hobbes, Kant, Montesquieu, Clausewitz, Lenin, the neo-realism of Kenneth Waltz, the constructivism of Alexander Wendt, the economic approach of Paul Collier, and peace research trends. These are, in Weberian terms, *ideal types*. They all structure the contemporary thought of war and disclose its main features. Through the analysis of these approaches, light will be shed on their biases. These views limit the understanding of war, notably because they conceal the potential reconfiguration that could happen within war. They imply a simplification and a reduction of the complexity of war, and thus a difficulty in grasping war as multi-dimensional, complex, and productive.

Part II, in contrast to the theories previously analyzed, explains and conceptualizes war as a generative social phenomenon, both uncertain and complex. This part expounds on how war is a space-time in which groups experience processes of construction and deconstruction of themselves, their environment, and their relationships; it is a social phenomenon that destroys, creates, and feeds identities. Rather than as a tool or a fixed event, war must be understood as a CAS.

This hypothesis will be supported, in Part III, by two examples: the Second Congo War (1998-2003) and the Vietnam War until the end of US involvement (1954-1973). It will demonstrate that war is not fixed to an immutable political plan. War is, rather, a complex sequence of actions in constant motion. Its multi-dimensionality means that reasons of war change throughout war – one can start to fight for one reason, continue to fight for another one, and end for yet a different one. It will be explained how both of these wars, Congo and

Vietnam, were CAS. They were such spaces of change that they impacted the evolution of the purpose of war itself.

For clarity, the scope of this work as well as its limits must be outlined. Firstly, this research does not intend to neglect the relevance of previous definitions and conceptions of war. Secondly, it does not aim to propose a new definition of war. Thirdly, it can be argued that this research considers war as a natural, innate, or uncontrollable feature of living as part of a community because this work criticizes the contemporary tendency to think of war as something that must be justified, legitimate, or obedient to a political reason.[7] But the purpose of this work is not to assess these considerations, which result from ideological choices or opinions.

This research aims to propose a conceptual framework, a perspective that can allow one to grasp war differently on the philosophical, political, and strategic levels. This outlook is not inevitably in opposition to other definitions. It looks to give back to war its dimensions, to outline its thickness and the complexity of what happens within it. This is why it will avoid starting with a definition of war, in order to not confine the research and to bring out its protean and complex nature. The debate on the definition of war is complex in its own right. It concerns just a definition, which is nothing but a term that tries to grasp a reality. Nonetheless, the definition process itself can be instrumentalized; in other words, to define something as war can be done on purpose in order to achieve specific aims. All this points out the limitations of the definition. That said, this research will be based on a comprehension of war simply as a period of collective and organized violence in which warring parties' life is at play.

Putting aside the issue of the correct word for a specific reality, this research aims to better understand some of its

---

[7] The importance of legitimization in contemporary international affairs goes in this direction. International law and the UN are used to legitimate actions – whether one considers these kinds of systems and organizations as efficient or not. Countries demonstrate a will to justify their wars to the world, the media, and public opinion.

mechanisms. It goes beyond a strict definition to enter into the phenomenon, the reality, which is complex and nuanced; it wants to go where theory and practice are in struggle and at work. Clausewitz distinguished "absolute war" that tends toward extremes from real war that responds to politics and compromises. He substituted an absolute and unreal war for another unreal war. The reality of war is more atypical, nuanced, and full of new developments. It is this complex, uncertain, and changing space-time that is explored here. The book aims to avoid the tendency to think of war as one in its structure, trajectory, project, and pattern. It grasps war as a space-time oriented by an inertia that is both linked to the past as well as in perpetual mutation and rebuilding.

PART I

THE SIMPLIFICATION AND REDUCTION OF WAR CONCEPTUALIZATION

CHAPTER 1
CLASSIC CONCEPTIONS OF WAR

In this chapter, the thoughts of Hobbes, Kant, Montesquieu, Machiavelli, Clausewitz, and Lenin are expounded. These authors are chosen because they structure the contemporary thought of war. As suggested by Hans-Georg Gadamer, we can hope to understand the terms by which we are preoccupied only if we see in it our own questions;[8] in other words, "we search for answers to our own questions."[9] Thus, beyond what these theories openly state about war, the way they raise the issue of war matters.

Firstly, the chapter presents the theories of Hobbes, Kant, and Montesquieu, for whom war is mainly thought of as a part of a wider conception, of a whole system. Hobbes and Kant represent respectively the fathers of realism and liberalism. Montesquieu, although less influential in the field, is equally interesting, as he raises the issue of war through the same perspective as Kant and Hobbes but in a different way. Secondly, Machiavelli and Clausewitz are presented as advocates of instrumental war – war as a tool or means. Thirdly, it is shown how revolutionary war has been thought of by communists such as Lenin, expressly as a means to achieve a greater good.

---

[8] *cf.* "Nous ne pouvons espérer comprendre les énoncés qui nous occupent que dans la mesure où nous y reconnaissons nos propres questions." Hans-Georg Gadamer, *Langage et Vérité*, trans. Jean-Claude Gens (Paris: Gallimard, 1995), 251.

[9] Hans-Georg Gadamer, "Towards a Phenomenology of Ritual and Language," in *Language and Linguisticality in Gadamer's Hermeneutics*, ed. Lawrence K. Schmidt (Lanham: Lexington Books, 2000), 42.

Toward Peace: Hobbes, Kant and Montesquieu

Hobbes

It is manifest that during the time men live without a common power to keep them all in awe, they are in that condition which is called war; and such a war as is of every man against every man.[10]

– Thomas Hobbes

War is normal, according to Hobbes. In the English philosopher's view, men are naturally at war. He does not try to legitimize war, he simply states a fact: "The notions of right and wrong, justice and injustice, have there no place. Where there is no common power, there is no law; where no law, no injustice."[11] Nevertheless, men fear death and desire commodious living. Consequently, it makes them inclined toward peace.

From this axiom, Hobbes develops an entire system of rules, laws, and organizations that could guarantee peace at best. The organization of society is what matters the most, and war is only the starting point of Hobbes' reasoning. This is what Pierre Hassner points out: "Chez Hobbes, chez Locke et chez Kant, comme dans toute la tradition libérale, le but de la politique est le même: garantir la paix…"[12] Everything starts with the fact that men are born almost equal in the faculties of body and mind. "From this equality of ability ariseth equality of hope in the attaining of our ends"[13] – therefore, if two men desire the same thing they cannot both have, they become

---

[10] Thomas Hobbes, *Leviathan* (London: Penguin Classics, 1985), 185.
[11] *Ibid.*, 188.
[12] Pierre Hassner, "Les Concepts de Guerre et de Paix chez Kant," *Revue Française de science politique* 11, no.3 (1961), 646.
[13] Hobbes, *Leviathan*, 184.

adversaries. As Doyne Dawson[14] observes, Hobbes starts with a deterministic assumption about human nature, which is that all people are uniformly egoistic, controlled by an *animus dominandi* comprising three passions – competition, diffidence, and glory – which puts them eternally at odds with one another. Therefore, unless they find a way to coexist under the authority and the domination of a supreme power – the Leviathan – there will be war of all against all, more precisely a situation of permanent danger and potential struggle. Hobbes does not consider war as a tool or instrument. War is natural. Wars happen ordinarily if people do not manage to live at peace.

On the whole, the author of *Leviathan* has a very broad and open conception of war. War is the situation of threat and potential struggle between men that arises when there is no sovereign authority.

> For war consisteth not in battle only, or the act of fighting, but in a tract of time, wherein the will to contend by battle is sufficiently known: and therefore the notion of time is to be considered in the nature of war, as it is in the nature of weather. For as the nature of foul weather lieth not in a shower or two of rain, but in an inclination thereto of many days together: so the nature of war consisteth not in actual fighting, but in the known disposition thereto during all the time there is no assurance to the contrary. All other time is peace.[15]

Hobbes comprehends the time dimension of war as well as its uncertainty, which is central in making it dangerous. However, war is not at the center of his purpose; social order is. War takes the back seat. Overall, it is what allows him to comment on peace and to build a theory on the organization of society that includes commentary on politics, laws, rules, authority, control, etc.

---

[14] Dawson Doyne, "The Origins of War: Biological and Anthropological Theories," *History and Theory* 35, no.1 (1996):3.
[15] Hobbes, *Leviathan*, 185-186.

To conclude on Hobbes, the issue of war is the main starting point of his argument. By explaining that threat and danger are contained in war as opposed to peace, he proposes a system to guarantee social order. Michel Foucault remarked that "it is as though, far from being the theorist of the relationship between war and political power, Hobbes wanted to eliminate the historical reality of war."[16] What war means socially and politically is denied. Hobbes turns "war, the fact of war and the relationship of force that is actually manifested in the battle, into something that has nothing to do with the constitution of sovereignty."[17] It is purely a social contract theory that is mainly focused on the contractual aspect to reach stability and which neglects transitions, changes, and uncertainty, and thus the multi-dimensionality of wars.

Kant

How to achieve peace? This is the main issue, according to Immanuel Kant, as underlined by the title of his famous essay *Perpetual Peace*. War must ideally be avoided, knowing that peace between men is the greatest and ultimate good. However, for Kant, war does at times occur and must be understood, in the big picture, as a transitional moment in the course of history toward peace. Even if Kant is known to be an idealist at the origins of political liberalism, his thought remains complex and nuanced. Pierre Hassner remarkably synthesizes it through the following sentence: "Kant croit plus à la guerre et croit plus à la paix."[18] It means that, compared with other philosophers, war and peace are not just concepts for Kant, they are concrete phenomena. It is because war happens that peace will arise, both notions being connected. Kant understands the power and consequences of war.

---

[16] Michel Foucault, *Society Must Be Defended*, trans. David Macey (New York: Picador, 2003), 97.
[17] *Ibid.*, 97.
[18] Hassner, *Concepts*, 652. Translation: "Kant believes more in war and believes more in peace."

In *Idea for a Universal History from a Cosmopolitan Point of View*, Kant presents war as both a negative phenomenon to avoid and a necessary evil leading to a supreme consciousness. From one standpoint, man is endowed with natural capacities that he must practice and improve. From the other, he speculates that everything is ordered by what he calls Nature or Providence. Ultimately, man must confront ordeals of Nature and use this to improve himself. "Reason itself does not work instinctively, but requires trial, practice, and instruction in order gradually to progress from one level of insight to another."[19] Like reason, struggles between men are a part of the pathway toward order: expressly, they are a test. According to Kant, this complementarity between conflict and social order is possible thanks to "the unsocial sociability of men."[20] Man has both an inclination to enter into society and a propensity to isolate himself from others. However, it is through this opposition that men improve their condition.

> Without those in themselves unamiable characteristics of unsociability from whence opposition springs – characteristics each man must find in his own selfish pretensions – all talents would remain hidden, unborn in an Arcadian shepherd's life, with all its concord, contentment, and mutual affection... Without them, all the excellent natural capacities of humanity would forever sleep, undeveloped... The natural urges to this, the sources of unsociableness and mutual opposition from which so many evils arise, drive men to new exertions of their forces and thus to the manifold development of their capacities.[21]

Progressively, Kant builds an analogy between the individual and the group. In the seventh thesis, he pushes the analogy further by extending it to the international level. Hence,

---

[19] Immanuel Kant, "Idea for a Universal History from a Cosmopolitan Point of View," in *On History*, trans. Lewis White Beck (Indianapolis: Bobbs-Merrill, 1963), 13.
[20] *Ibid.*, 15.
[21] *Ibid.*, 15.

war becomes the sign of Nature. War is a step on the process toward perpetual peace.

> All wars are accordingly so many attempts (not in the intention of man, but in the intention of Nature) to establish new relations among states, and through the destruction or at least the dismemberment of all of them to create new political bodies.[22]

In Kant's thought, if men have to focus on something, it is rather on looking for peace than on analyzing war. From the human point of view, war is not entirely its concern because he does not really control it. War is only a moment that can help men to practice and ameliorate their reason and their behavior. Kant is like Hobbes because he does not consider that war is a tool. Kant rather considers it as a necessary moment if it happens. War must not be desired; however, if it arises, it is only a step toward peace. War is natural for Hobbes and necessary for Kant. For both authors, war is a part of the natural order of things. However, both are looking to pass over it in order to achieve the most peaceful situation possible.

Céline Acker explains how Kant is more thetic than descriptive about war. Kantian philosophy seems to be written for the audience rather than for the players.[23] What matters for Kant is not war in itself; within a larger framework, its dimension, its uncertainty, its productivity, and what happens in it does not really matter. Following Kant's perspective, war must be understood through the bigger picture, as a step toward perpetual peace, as a part of a whole.

---

[22] *Ibid.*, 18-19.
[23] Céline Acker, "La 'scène' de la guerre ou la monstration des mécanismes chez Eschyle et Kant," *Sens Public* (Feburary 2002).

Montesquieu

As soon as man enters into a state of society he loses the sense of his weakness; equality ceases, and then commences the state of war.[24]

– Charles de Secondat Montesquieu

Montesquieu conceives of war as a durable moment, similarly to Hobbes. Revolution and invasion are not war, war is a persisting conflictual state. There are two different states of war that both follow the same logic. Naturally, people are not at war because they feel weak. When they begin to live together, expressly in a state of society, war starts because they feel strong. This is the first kind of war. The same logic produces war between nations. Each society progressively feels stronger, which induces conflict between them. This is the second kind of war. Ultimately, this parallelism between conflicts of individuals and conflicts of societies is temporary, as suggests Jean Terrel.[25] It is mostly the second kind of war, *i.e.*, between societies, that persists. Each nation fights for its conservation. Said differently, war allows one to preserve society's interests – interests that must be materialized into the *law of nations*.

> The object of war is victory; that of victory is conquest; and that of conquest preservation. From this and the preceding principle all those rules are derived which constitute the *law of nations*.[26]

The interests of each society, each nation, vary. Consequently, war between nations will probably remain. Hence, war is not the issue for the French philosopher. Rules and laws are what matter, more than war. Indeed, Montesquieu grasps war as a means to achieve a greater end, as underlined by

---

[24] Charles de Secondat Montesquieu, *The Spirit of Laws* (New York: Cosimo, 2007), 5.
[25] Jean Terrel, "Guerre," in *Dictionnaire électronique Montesquieu* (February 2008), http://dictionnaire-montesquieu.ens-lyon.fr/index.php?id=362.
[26] Montesquieu, *Spirit of Laws*, 5.

Jean Terrel: "Montesquieu fait de la guerre un moyen au profit d'une fin qui lui est supérieure, en évitant cependant le lyrisme de la paix et le pathétique des misères de la guerre."[27]

       For Montesquieu, there is no war without society, there is no society without war.[28] So, war does not exist in the state of nature, and it cannot be overcome or substituted by a universal legal space, in contrast to Kant. Even if Montesquieu paradoxically considers war as an "aberration,"[29] in the end, it is for him a regular process of preservation from which the law of nations can be constituted. Like Hobbes and Kant but in another way, Montesquieu does not linger very much on war. War is not studied because it is a permanent feature. At the end, what matters much more is how to organize society.

       To conclude, for Hobbes, Kant, and Montesquieu, war is not studied in itself and for itself. None of them examine the complexity and plurality of war. They use war in order to understand human nature, and then to set up the best system possible to improve the human condition. The three authors are oriented toward peace rather than war. For Hobbes, war is a state that proves what human nature is, and that makes necessary a specific organization of society. For Kant, it is ineffective to spend time studying war because what matters is how to achieve peace and avoid war. If war happens sometimes, it must be understood as part of a long-term process that nobody can directly change. According to Montesquieu, war is inextricably linked to society and cannot be eradicated. Therefore, war being inevitable, discussing it will not bring any solutions. On the contrary, he is more focused on rules and laws of society because they are adjustable. None of the three philosophers gives any space to uncertainty; war is a natural crossing-point in the order of things. All try to justify war by explaining either its reasons or what results from it. They neglect its proper dimensions.

---

[27] Jean Terrel, "Paix," in *Dictionnaire électronique Montesquieu* (February 2008), http://dictionnaire-montesquieu.ens-lyon.fr/index.php?id=363.
[28] *Ibid.*
[29] Martin van Creveld, *The Transformation of War* (New York: Free Press, 1991), 124.

War as a Tool: Machiavelli and Clausewitz

Machiavelli

Niccolò Machiavelli is known as the founding father of modern politics. He does not focus on what politics should be or if there is an ultimate benefit. On the contrary, his concern is about how to deal with reality. Ideals and morality are not disregarded, but Machiavelli makes a distinction between goals where morality and ideals matter, and means where they are ineffective. Too many "have imagined republics and principalities that have never been seen or known to exist in truth,"[30] and they neglect what is done for what ought to be done. Ultimately, what matters to Machiavelli, as Frédéric Gros[31] suggests, is to command, not to want.

Machiavelli represents a new step in political philosophy, as indicated by Martin van Creveld: "From Hugo Grotius, if not from Machiavelli, western political thought has defined war as an instrument in the hand of states; that is, of sovereign political entities recognizing no law and no judge above themselves."[32]

> A Prince ought to have no other aim or thought, nor select anything else for his study, than war and its rules and discipline; for this is the sole art that belongs to him who rules, and it is of such force that it not only upholds those who are born princes, but it often enables men to rise from a private station to that rank. And, on the contrary, it is seen that when princes have thought more of ease than of arms they have lost their states. And the first cause of your losing it is to neglect this art; and

---

[30] Niccolò Machiavelli, *The Prince*, trans. Harvey C. Mansfield (Chicago: University of Chicago, 1998), 61.
[31] Frédéric Gros, *Etats de violence: essai sur la fin de la guerre* (Paris: Gallimard, 2006), 121.
[32] Creveld, *Transformation of War*, 126.

what enables you to acquire a state is to be master of the art.[33]

For Machiavelli, politics is about having the right strategies and techniques for the circumstances. The moral issue is not in the first instance of political concern because politics is about power and authority. In this way, war is nothing more than a tool that the prince can use; it is neither good nor bad.

Concerning the conduct of war, Machiavelli is aware of its uncertainty, the world on the whole, and thus war, being half determined by what he calls *fortuna*. But men have to work with the other half, the one that depends on their free will. In the end, Machiavelli is not interested in the uncertain and undeterminable part of the reality; what matters is to take action.

To conclude, Machiavelli's approach to war is purely instrumentalized and goal-oriented. Even if he understands the uncertainty of war, this must not hinder any action. Finally, war is rationalized because it is understood as a tool and because the focus is only put on strategies to win.

Clausewitz

Carl von Clausewitz (1780-1831), a general in the Prussian army, is central to our purpose. Indeed, he is one of the most famous authors of the articulation between war and politics. Clausewitz made an attempt to conciliate the political reason for war and the caprices of its conduct. Ultimately, he subordinates war to politics, in line with the rhetoric of mainstream strategic thought that considered war as rationalistic, instrumentalized, and organized by nature.[34]

---

[33] Machiavelli, *The Prince*, 58.
[34] *cf.* Creveld, *Transformation of War*, 160.

Firstly, what is war in itself, in its basic form and without any consideration of its purpose, according to Clausewitz?

> War in its literal meaning is fighting, for fighting alone is the efficient principle in the manifold activity which, in a wide sense, is called war. But fighting is a trial of strength of the moral and physical forces by means of the latter.[35]

War, therefore, is an act of violence to compel our opponent to fulfill our will.[36]

If wars are all fighting and share this common premise, they are not the same across time and space. Clausewitz considers change as a part of war; it is a "true chameleon"[37] because its form changes according to the context.

Clausewitz argues that war is made up of a trinity "composed of the original violence of its elements, hatred and animosity, which may be looked upon as blind instinct; of the play of probabilities and chance, which make it a free activity of the soul; and of the subordinate nature of a political instrument, by which it belongs purely to the reason."[38] Through this trinity, Clausewitz apprehends war as this complex mix, and not only as a political instrument.

That said, politics occupies a much bigger place in his conception of war than what is suggested before. In *On War*, Clausewitz asserts that war, like everything in social reality, is not absolute; it is neither totally rational nor totally irrational; it is an "in between." In this context, he does not ignore the uncertainty of war. However, like Machiavelli, uncertainty is of no help – it is even counterproductive to his argument; it is thus consigned to be one among the many features of war. According to Clausewitz, in the reality of war, things ultimately

---

[35] Carl V. Clausewitz, *On War: The Complete edition*, trans. Colonel J.J. Graham (Rockville: Wildside Press, 2009), 52-53.
[36] *Ibid.*, 13.
[37] *Ibid.*, 25.
[38] *Ibid.*, 25.

take a direction and have meaning; politics eventually intercedes and leads war according to its meaning and its reasons. In the end, the fact that war changes and is affected by chance, subjectivity, and emotions does not make it totally contradictory to its political and rational aspects. War is politics at the level of its purpose. Politics, which leads the society, underpins war; it is its thread. Thus, one can understand why war is nothing more than a continuation of politics. Politics is the thought, war is the instrument. "Thus, the political object, as the original motive of the war, will be the standard for determining both the aim of the military force, and also the amount of effort to be made."[39]

Typical of his epoch, Clausewitz considers that war is an instrument of the state. His thought is state-centric. This is explained by Creveld, who is very critical of Clausewitz's political conception of war, stating that, for Clausewitz, the only organized violence that can be named "war" is engaged by the state, for the state, and against the state.[40] War would be unjust if it were not guided by a political reason, that of the state. Ariel Colonomos indirectly underlines the same idea, stating that, in Clausewitz's epoch, the Prince is at war on behalf of a reason, a *Kriegraison*, which is the assertion of the reason of the state.[41] This Clausewitzian perception is still widely shared by many western minds.

To conclude, war is essentially a political tool for Clausewitz. In his attempt to conciliate the political reason for war and the caprices of its conduct, he explains both. But ultimately, the political reason gets the upper hand – meaning that Clausewitz is either idealistic, *i.e.*, war only obeys a political reason, or prescriptive, *i.e.*, war must obey a political reason. For Clausewitz does not put in the foreground the fact that war may have its own dimensions, changes, and purposes. Creveld defined him as a "philospher in uniform" who must be

---

[39] Clausewitz, *On War*, 18.
[40] Creveld, *Transformation of War*, 36.
[41] Ariel Colonomos, *La Pari de la guerre: Guerre préventive, guerre juste?* (Paris: Denoël, 2009), 116.

understood in the rationalistic, scientific, and technological context of his epoch.[42] In a way, for Clausewitz, war is logical, organized, and rational; war is and must be political.

Whereas Hobbes, Kant, and Montesquieu were looking at war as a part of a wider pathway toward a better situation like peace, Machiavelli and Clausewitz grasp war as an instrument. The internal aspects of war can be uncertain and complicated. This is, however, a technical detail relegated to tactics and eventually strategy. Globally, war is a tool, which is by essence and must stay oriented and guided by politics. Ultimately, what matters for both of these "philosophers" is how to run a war in order to achieve one's will; the rest is without real interest.

The Use of Conflict Through the Perspective of Historical Materialism: Lenin's Wars and Revolutions

The history of all hitherto existing society is the history of class struggles.[43]

– Karl Marx

The communist perspective on war is important because it shaped a substantial part of the world's thinking in the second half of the twentieth century. Vladimir Ilyich Lenin's thought on war is analyzed because during this period he was one of the few who developed a structured communist perspective on war.

Lenin clearly puts himself in the tradition of Clausewitz by putting war as consubstantial to politics. This is what he explains in a lecture delivered on May 14, 1917:

> War is a continuation of policy by other means. All wars are inseparable from the political systems that

---

[42] Creveld, *Transformation of War*, 64.
[43] Karl Marx and Friedrich Engels, *Manifesto of the Communist Party* (New York: Cosimo Classics, 2009), 39.

engender them. The policy which a given state, a given class within that state, pursued for a long time before the war is inevitably continued by that same class during the war, the form of action alone being changed.[44]

Lenin is not of this "category of people who are unqualified opponents to all wars,"[45] although he does not consider it a game. War is an evil that has been brought by the ruling classes and only a revolution of the working class can end it. Thus, revolutions must be fought in order to achieve a socialist system of society which, by eliminating the division of mankind into classes, by eliminating all exploitation of man by man and nation by nation, will inevitably eliminate the very possibility of war. In a more subtle way, Lenin is like the Marxist author Emmanuel Kanter. For him, civilization as a whole is a society of war because it is a society of private property; whereas communism would be the "Society of Peace and Happiness." According to Kanter, the gradual accumulation of capital and private property intensifies wars and revolutions. In other words, capitalism caused the degeneracy of society toward barbarism, and the only way to find peace again is communism through revolution.[46]

Elsewhere, Lenin presents a new step in communist thought on international relations through his perspective on colonialism. According to Marx, colonialism is a necessary evil that could allow class struggles to spread, which could then lead to an international revolution. On the contrary, Lenin argues that colonialism results from imperialist capitalism. He develops a clear link between class struggles and the international situation. At the national and international level, struggles have the same source. For Lenin, capitalism contains in itself the seeds of international struggles because the supreme stage of capitalism is imperialism: "Imperialism emerged as the

---

[44] Vladimir I. Lenin, "War and Revolution," in *Lenin: Collected Works*, vol.24:398-421 (Moscow: Progress Publishers, 1964).
[45] *Ibid.*
[46] Emanual Kanter, *The Evolution of War: A Marxian Study* (Chicago: Charles H. Kerr & Company, 1927), 118-123.

development and direct continuation of the fundamental characteristics of capitalism in general."[47]

In Lenin's approach, as in most communist ones, there is a difference between civil, national, and international wars and revolutionary wars. If one focuses on revolutions, they are understood by Lenin as a necessary violence in order to achieve the more peaceful situation of the communist society. In this way, revolutionary wars are, like for Machiavelli and Clausewitz, a tool serving a political purpose. This violence is clearly an instrument of an ideology. Similarly to Kant, this takes place in a historical materialistic but idealistic perspective: specifically, revolutionary wars are necessary tools toward freedom. As opposed to revolutions, wars are like diseases related to capitalistic societies. Nothing productive really happens in war.

In the end, war is, for Lenin, mainly understood as an instrument used in class struggles. As Walter Bryce Gallie observes,[48] conflict is not rejected in general as inherently evil or irrational; conflicts fought to liberate suppressed classes and races are approved, expressly revolutionary wars. What is important is to achieve a communist society, which will be peaceful by essence. In order to do this, revolutionary wars are necessary.

To conclude this chapter, two main tendencies in comprehending war can be identified. On the one hand, there are authors such as Hobbes, Kant, and Montesquieu, who focus on the overall system, its organization and rules, but not so much on war itself. War is a mere cog in a bigger framework. Globally, war is the support that allows them to propose a set of prescriptions including specific behaviors, actions, or structures. On the other hand, there are those who have an instrumental reading of war, such as Clausewitz, Machiavelli, and Lenin.

---

[47] Vladimir I. Lenin, *Imperialism, the Highest Stage of Capitalism: A Popular Outline*, 3rd ed. (Beijing: Foreign Languages Press, 1970), 104.
[48] Walter B. Gallie, *Philosophers of Peace and War: Kant, Clausewitz, Marx, Engels and Tolstoy* (Cambridge: Cambridge University Press, 1978), 74.

War is a means, a tool that serves more important purposes, such as politics.

Both of these tendencies are teleological, because war is turned toward a specific goal. Among them, most of the authors tend to be prescriptive, because they give rules and directions to follow. War is fixed and condemned to have a limited place or role. Its own dimension is not analyzed. War is not understood as a phenomenon. This restricts our knowledge of its complexity, generativeness, change, uncertainty, and autonomy.

CHAPTER 2
CONTEMPORARY PERSPECTIVES

Now that classical theories on war since the beginning of "political modernity" have been discussed, this chapter will broach more contemporary theories. It will be shown that, even if war's dimensions are sometimes better understood, there is still a trend to reduce war and understand it in a teleological way. The neo-realism of Kenneth Waltz, the constructivism of Alexander Wendt, political economic perspectives, and finally peace research and conflict resolution approaches are presented.

The International System Induces War: The Neo-Realism of Kenneth Waltz

Kenneth Waltz is known as one of the founders of the neo-realist, or structural realist, school. It is through his books *Man, the State, and War*, published in 1959, and *Theory of International Politics*, published in 1979, that he presented the tenets of his theory, which "remains a touchstone for both realists and their critics."[49] In short, it is called structural realism or neo-realism because, firstly, the international scene is understood as an anarchical one, which is typical from the realism perspective; and secondly, it is the structure of the international system itself which makes it anarchical and not human nature or the nature of the state. There are wars because nothing prevents them from happening. In the end, war is, for Waltz, of limited interest in itself; war is a part of a whole system, and helps us understand the features of this system.

---

[49] Jack Donnelly, *Realism and International Relations Theory* (Cambridge: Cambridge University Press, 2000), 16.

In *Man, the State, and War*, Waltz's purpose concerns "how to think about war and peace."[50] In order to understand international politics and the relations between its actors, Waltz examines past conceptions of war in terms of cause and remedy. He seeks to understand how past theorists apprehended war, particularly in terms of origins.

To describe and classify these theories, he uses three "images" that correspond to three levels of analysis of war's roots. The first "image" is the one of authors who consider the origins of war within human nature and individual behavior. According to this perspective, reasons of war must be found within men; in other words, war is a result of who men are and how they act. The second "image" is the one of authors who consider the origins of war within the internal structure of states; more precisely, what causes war relates to the structure of the state in question, like the kind of regime it has or its foreign policy. The third "image" is the most valuable for Waltz, even if they are complementary in *Man, the State, and War*. It considers that wars are due to the international system; in other words, the international system has such characteristics that it is in a state of anarchy, which makes war inevitable. This image corresponds to the new perspective Waltz brings to the international relations field.

> With many sovereign states, with no system of law enforceable among them, with each state judging its grievances and ambitions according to the dictates of its own reason or desire – conflict, sometimes leading to war, is bound to occur.[51]

As a result of the structure and features of the international scene, wars always occur. By drawing up these three categories, Waltz classifies not only war conceptions but international relations theories too. It allows him to conclude with a general statement about the "reality" of international

---

[50] Kenneth N. Waltz, *Man, the State, and War*, 2nd revised ed. (New York: Columbia University Press, 2001), 2.
[51] *Ibid.*, 159.

politics. By proposing a new way to see international relations, he actually supports and legitimates a certain way to act and behave on the international scene.

> Each state pursues its own interest, however defined, in ways it judges best. Force is a means of achieving the external ends of states because there exists no consistent, reliable process of reconciling the conflicts of interest that inevitably arise among similar units in a condition of anarchy. A foreign policy based on this image of international relations is neither moral nor immoral, but embodies merely a reasoned response to the world about us.[52]

Waltz is practically oriented and tends to be prescriptive. What matters for him is to analyze and describe the international system's features in order to establish a set of behavioral rules. Waltz uses war as a starting point to understand politics. Thus, even if Waltz's book is devoted to the causes of war, his *focus is not primarily on war* but on the international system and its practices. Consequently, like Hobbes, Kant, and Montesquieu, dimensions, uncertainty, and productivity of war do not really matter; what matters is the overall system.

War Is What States Make of It: The Constructivist Perspective

Constructivism was born to propose a new perspective in the international relations debate. As Thomas Lindemann says, the core paradigm of this theory resides in "its opposition to 'fixed' theories of rational choice according to which actors' preferences would be stable."[53] The choice that a state can make between military force, economic well-being, or the defense of

---

[52] *Ibid.*, 238.
[53] Thomas Lindemannn, *Causes of War: The Struggle for Recognition* (Colchester: ECPR Press, 2010), 22.

human rights is variable and "depends in particular upon the identity reference framework within the international community."[54]

Constructivists bring a focus on inter-subjectivity, in contrast to realism or liberalism, which tend to focus on materialistic aspects. Identity and recognition are at the forefront. Alexander Wendt, the standard-bearer of constructivism, synthesizes it in the following passage from one of his most famous articles:

> I argue that self-help and power politics do not follow either logically or causally from anarchy and that if today we find ourselves in a self-help world, this is due to process, not structure. There is no 'logic' of anarchy apart from the practices that create and instantiate one structure of identities and interests rather than another; structure has no existence or causal powers apart from process… Anarchy is what states make of it.[55]

Consequently, the interests of states and other actors vary because of the evolution of the corresponding norms and identities. Thus, for Wendt, for instance, it is not the state of the nature of the international system that makes it anarchical, but it is international actors' perceptions and subsequent actions.

Constructivism gets out of the rational approach to war, understands war as a social phenomenon, and apprehends the notion of variation. That said, the main focus is put on causes of war – specifically, "why war." This reduces the field of analysis because it remains on the boundaries of war. Internal variations and complexity are not taken into account. Finally, like Hobbes, Kant, Montesquieu, and Waltz, what matters for constructivists is the overall system and its features. The focus is not primarily put on war, which is merely a symptom. Dario Battistella suggests that constructivism is finally a way to

---

[54] *Ibid.*, 22.
[55] Alexander Wendt, "Anarchy is What States Make of It: The Social Construction of Power Politics," *International Organization* 46, no.2 (1992), 394-395.

study all social relations. Hence, it is more a social theory to which one can apply an international relations theory than an international relations theory in itself.[56] Even if this theory is very influential in the international relations debate, it confirms the lack of a dynamic, dimensional, and complex understanding of war in current theorizations.

War and Economics

Since the 1970s, a new movement called international political economy has developed out of an initiative by Susan Strange.[57] Its aim was to take up the political economy tradition of Aristotle, David Ricardo, Marx, *et al.*, in order to grasp the new dynamics of international affairs. More precisely, the idea was to decompartmentalize both international economy and international relations, because world affairs could no longer be comprehended with pure political theories. According to this perspective, if one wants to understand war's dynamics in the current globalized world, an economic lens is essential.

Paul Collier follows this tradition. He is known for his economic analysis of war. Focusing mainly on "Third World" conflicts, Collier proposes a new way to grasp the dynamics of civil war. According to him, the real challenge is that there is a "group of countries at the bottom that are falling behind, and often falling apart."[58] His aim is to understand the logics of these intractable situations in order to propose "a range of policy instruments to encourage the countries of the bottom billion to take steps toward change."[59] At the outset, he

---

[56] Dario Battistella, *Théories des relations internationales*, 2nd ed. (Paris: Presses de la Fondation nationale des sciences politiques, 2006), 286.
[57] *Ibid.*, 427-456.
[58] Paul Collier, *The Bottom Billion: Why the Poorest Countries are Failing and What Can Be Done About It* (New York: Oxford University Press, 2008), 3.
[59] *Ibid.*, 12.

considers that rebellion is "an ultimate manifestation of organized crime."[60] The rebels are actually predators.

> There is a profound gap between popular perceptions of the causes of conflict and the results from recent economic analysis. Popular perceptions see rebellion as a protest motivated by genuine and extreme grievance. Rebels are public-spirited heroes fighting against injustice. Economic analysis sees rebellion as more like a form of organized crime, or more radically, as something that is better understood from the distinctive circumstances in which it is feasible, rather than worrying about what might motivate its participants.[61]

According to Collier's economic theory of conflicts, the motivation of conflict is unimportant; what is more significant is whether the rebels can sustain themselves financially. In other words, it is the feasibility of predation that determines the risk of conflict.[62] Rebels behave like predators, which survive as a result of war. The more potential wealth that can be found in war, the more likely war is to happen.

The importance given to economics in many war theories of that kind is tied to the fact that economics is considered to play a key role, if not the main role, in the contemporary globalized world. This economic-based approach to war re-emerged for various reasons. Firstly, there is the global context that includes globalization, the end of the Cold War, the liberalization of the world, the growth of the free market, and international communications systems and interconnectedness. Secondly, there is the fact that many conflicts happen in underdeveloped or developing regions in

---

[60] Paul Collier, "Economic Causes of Civil Conflict and their Implications in Policy," in *Leashing the Dogs of War: Conflict Management in a Divided World*, ed. Chester Crocker, Fen Osler Hampson, and Pamela Aall (Washington, DC: United States Institute of Peace, 2008), 198.
[61] *Ibid.*, 197.
[62] *Ibid.*, 199.

which political purposes of war are apparently hard to grasp coherently. Therefore, the understanding of these conflicts through an economic spectrum has been attractive, as war would be a tool of economic interests.

If one takes the example of the Democratic Republic of the Congo, one can read the entire conflictual history of this country through an economic perspective. Natural resources have played a key role since colonization – at the end of the nineteenth century – until the 2000s. However, in contrast to colonization and the Cold War, which offered political keys for understanding, it is especially true in contemporary times that natural resources seem to be at the forefront. Currently, there is no single clear or apparent political line driving the conflict; there is rather a permanent tense and complex situation in which economic resources can be perceived as fueling the conflict or creating it – hence the attractiveness of an economic perspective on these kinds of conflict.[63] This economic approach has the credit of underlining what is happening throughout and inside war. The focus is put on the internal reasons causing war. War is a system in which some groups blossom. Thereby, the conflict is considered as a social space in which people carry out or lose their business.

However, there is a threefold problem with this approach to war. Firstly, it is unidimensional; consequently, there is a kind of self-blindness. War would be only about money. The purely economic focus prevents one from elaborating complex and multiple approaches. Secondly, war is globally considered as negative. The economics of war is denounced as the main cause of conflicts. Thirdly, war is considered as a tool. Warfare would be mainly an instrument – of money, to be specific. This instrumentalization of war, as with Machiavelli or Clausewitz, oversimplifies the analysis of it.

Consequently, even if this perspective grasps one important dimension of war in terms of space and time, it

---

[63] *cf.* Samuel Solvit, *RDC: Rêve ou illusion?* (Paris: L'Harmattan, 2009).

retains an economic bias that narrows the analytical spectrum. Warfare is reduced to a unique explanatory variable. Instead of the common trend to explain wars by politics, economic interests are placed at the forefront; but, the error is still the same, if not worse, because the complexity, the dimensions, and the social reality of war are once again denied. Economics must be understood as only one element among the many comprising the war phenomenon.

War as a Destructive Phenomenon: Peace Research and Conflict Resolution Studies

The purpose of our work goes beyond finding better ways of solving conflict. It involves a commitment to contribute to a better world.[64]

– Bernard Mayer

As a starting point, peace research and conflict resolution studies can be defined as follows: all the studies that develop an understanding of conflicts, their causes, and their mechanisms in order to bring conflicts to an end and to reach peace. In other words, they are all pieces of research focusing on how international violence can be prevented and how political control can be put in place for solving conflicts. The mere name of these fields is instructive concerning their perspective. Whatever it is called – peace research, conflict resolution, conflict management, or conflict transformation – all these names show their overall purpose, which is to end violence and achieve peaceful situations. Following the perspective of Oliver Ramsbotham, Tom Woodhouse, and Hugh Miall, conflict resolution is a "term which implies that deep-rooted sources of conflict are addressed and transformed. This implies that behavior is no longer violent, attitudes are no longer hostile, and the structure of the conflict has been changed... The term refers both to the process (or the

---

[64] *Ibid.*, 242.

intention) to bring about these changes, and to the completion of the process."[65] Conflict resolution is an integral part of work for development, social justice, and social transformation.[66]

Regarding their focus, peace research and conflict resolution studies explore the depths of war in order to understand its mechanisms. These theories comprehend that, if one wants to solve or avoid a conflict, numerous and complex dimensions of the situation must be overcome. In essence, these theories are looking at understanding the mechanisms creating or fueling the conflict; thus, they do not have any choice other than to enter into the time and space framework of the conflict and deal with its various aspects, *i.e.*, social, political, cultural, economic.

That said, peace research and conflict resolution studies are still limited in their understanding of the war phenomenon. They implicitly restrict their comprehension of war by considering it, in essence, as a problem to solve, a destructive and counterproductive process. And, as suggested by Herfried Münkler, a number of researchers on peace and conflict issues are like Kant; they "have developed the vision of a gradual disappearance of war on a world scale."[67] While they very often point out that conflict is inherent to social life and "not in itself a bad thing,"[68] what really matters is to solve the conflict. They are in essence practically oriented and goal-oriented. They pass judgment on war, and they give precepts on what must be done.

This initial position steers the analysis of war in a certain way: firstly, it implies a normative and prescriptive approach because it is based on initial value judgments and on the importance of the subsequent actions; secondly, war being perceived as a problem to solve, it indirectly stops the

---

[65] *Ibid.*, 29.
[66] *Ibid.*, 8.
[67] Münkler, *The New Wars*, 72.
[68] Bernard Mayer, *The Dynamics of Conflict Resolution* (San Francisco: Jossey-Bass, 2000), 24.

understanding of its complexity, generativeness, social aspect, and various dimensions. It is in this way that Koen Vlassenroot and Timothy Raeymaekers remark that "peacebuilders often see armed conflicts as an object of intervention rather than as a complex outcome of (foremost local) conflict dynamics."[69]

In conclusion to this first part, it can be established that all the approaches presented in Chapter 1 and Chapter 2, from Machiavelli to Lenin to peace research, grasp war in such a way that many of its features are neglected. When these theories do not want to control war, they give it an overall purpose embedded in the pathway of human evolution. In both cases, they are teleological and often normative. War is not analyzed by and for itself; war is integrated into a system, either as a tool or as a cog. In the end, war is the support that allows them to propose a set of prescriptions including specific behaviors, actions, or structures. They consequently reduce and fix war in terms of time, space, interaction, purpose, aim, or evolution. In all cases, wars are less classifiable and more complex than what these theories suggest. War is generative of a web of new events, relationships, and effects. Hannah Arendt says that "action, though it may have a definite beginning, never as we shall see, has a predictable end"[70] because "each relationship established by action ends up in a web of ties and relationships, and thus always reaches out even further, setting much more into interconnected motion than the man who initiates action could ever have foreseen."[71]

The mix between explanatory and normative aspects of these theories is confusing. Whereas international relations are supposed to be explanatory, they are actually embedded

---

[69] Koen Vlassenroot and Timothy Raeymaekers, *The Formation of Centres of Profit, Power, and Protection: Conflict and Social Transformation in Eastern DR Congo*, Working paper (Janvier 2005), 1.
[70] Hannah Arendt, *The Human Condition*, 2nd ed. (London: University of Chicago Press, 1998), 144.
[71] Hannah Arendt, *The Promise of Politics* (New York: Schocken, 2005), 186-187.

within politics and history, which tends to make them normative too. In other words, international relations theories do not limit themselves to describing and explaining world affairs, they tend to give a direction, legitimize, or delegitimize some attitudes and say what should or should not be. Knowing that war studies tend to be encapsulated into or at least closely related to international relations studies, when one studies war, it becomes hard to clarify descriptive parts from normative ones. As this part shows, war often tends to be classified into a practically oriented political framework.

Thus, these theories must be understood in their context; they are embedded in the sociological, cultural, and political environment of their time. In *Society Must Be Defended*, Michel Foucault analyzes the evolution of war since the Middle Ages by pointing out its growing state-centric aspect. He explains that "with the growth and development of States throughout the Middle Ages and up to the threshold of the modern era, we see the practices and institutions of war undergoing a marked, very visible change."[72] This shift materialized through the fact that, gradually, only State powers could wage wars and manipulate the instruments of war; "the State acquired a monopoly of war."[73] The consequence of this State monopoly was "what might be called day-to-day warfare, and what was actually called 'private warfare', was eradicated from the social body, and from relations among men and relations among groups."[74] This analysis of the evolution of war enables one to put war theories into perspective; one can better grasp the context in which they emerged as well as the common way to think of war in the most recent centuries.

Arendt is equally enlightening in how war has been comprehended in the modern age. In *The Human Condition*, she differentiates between action and fabrication. Action is about the process itself, whereas fabrication is about the result.

---

[72] Foucault, *Society*, 48.
[73] *Ibid.*, 48.
[74] *Ibid.*, 48.

When men focus on action, it is the process of doing which matters; when men focus on fabrication, what matters is the result, the production, the end. She explains that the "substitution of making for acting...is as old as the tradition of political philosophy."[75] However, she points out how "the modern age defined man primarily as *homo faber*, a toolmaker and producer of things, and therefore could overcome the deep-seated contempt and suspicion in which the tradition had held the whole sphere of fabrication."[76] What happened is that "the modern age did not reverse the tradition but rather liberated it."[77]

Arendt's distinction allows us to understand how war has been theorized. War has globally and recently been thought of as a part of a "fabrication" process. For Machiavelli, Clausewitz, or Lenin, war is a way to fabricate a political result. According to the economic approaches, war is also understood as an instrument, but used for economic purposes. For Hobbes and Montesquieu, war brings out the need of political structures for human groups; thus, what matters is to fabricate this political structure and to minimize war. Waltz and Wendt use war as a cog in their argumentation; war helps them to understand the logic of international affairs and to set up some behavioral principles. For Kant, even if war is less about fabrication, it is still integrated in a goal-oriented process, which is partly controlled by men; so, the overall purpose is to do what is possible to move closer to peace. For peace research and conflict resolution studies, what matters is to understand war in order to control it and to produce a solution.

Ultimately, there is this strong belief that men master what happens around them.[78] These theories want to control war. As Foucault said, these perspectives of war are

---

[75] Arendt, *Human Condition*, 229.
[76] *Ibid.*, 229-230.
[77] *Ibid.*, 230.
[78] *Ibid.*, 144.

"something fragile and superficial...built on the top of this web of bodies, accidents, and passions."[79]

These theories are clearly biased. This is not a practical concern in itself until they affect contemporary political and strategic thoughts and lead them toward impasses. It is as if these thoughts do not grasp war any more, even the ones that are actually fought.

---

[79] Foucault, *Society*, 54-55.

PART II

A GENERATIVE SOCIAL PHENOMENON, UNCERTAIN AND SELF-MODIFYING

INTRODUCTION

Nous n'avons pas assisté au déroulement d'un plan mais aux improvisations d'un aventurier.[80]

– Raymond Aron

Don't matter who did what to who at this point. Fact is, we went to war and there ain't no turnin' back. I mean, s**t, it's what war is, you know? Once you in it, you in it. If it's a lie, then we fight on that lie. But we gotta fight.[81]

– Slim Charles, The Wire

In contrast to conceptualizing war as uniform and contracted, there is growing academic and military interest in considering war as a multiple and complex scene with limits that fade away. On the one hand, there are academics who study new forms that war can take, such as Nazih Richani with the notion of the "war system," and William Reno and Antonio Giustozzi with their analyses of warlordism. They point out the hybrid nature of war; war matures into something complex and vague. However, even if these authors have different theses and angles of research, they all underline the fact that many current wars are less state-centric, and less delimited in terms of political approach, aims, rules, time, and space. All these authors introduce some parts of contemporary conflicts' complexity and multiplicity. However, they present these two features – complexity and multiplicity – as consequences of warfare rather than as central matters defining war. On the other hand, military theorists are also aware of these features of war,

---

[80] Raymond Aron, *Les guerres en chaîne*, 3rd ed. (Paris: Gallimard, 1951), 51.
[81] *The Wire*, season III, episode 12, DVD, directed by David Simon (New York: HBO, 2006).

but they remain relegated to the background and considered as tactical or operational details that must not interfere with socio-political decisions or views.

In contrast to the theories presented in Part I and to these academic and military perspectives, the purpose of this part is to conceptualize war as a generative social phenomenon which is accordingly complex, uncertain, and self-modifying. The deepening of the understanding of war at the philosophical and political level begins with the awareness of its dimension, and thus of its generativeness, variations, autonomy, and complexity. Not only mere aspects of war among others, these features must be understood as defining elements of what war actually is.

Chapter 3 will explore dimensions of war in terms of time, space, and social interaction. Chapter 4 will focus on its subsequent productivity, which is connected to the notion of uncertainty and autonomy. Thereby, we will see how generative war is, especially in terms of politics. Chapter 5 will finally interpret war as a CAS.

For the purpose of clarity, this part essentially focuses on the theoretical aspects. It is completed by Part III, which brings in concrete examples to support the concept. The reason for this approach is that it is hard, if not impossible, to use particular examples without their context to back the theory. A war must be understood in its entire dynamics and thus presented as a whole; not doing so makes the complexity, the evolutions, and the generativeness of war harder to grasp.

CHAPTER 3
THE DIMENSIONS OF WAR

A Space-Time Construct

Spatial and temporal dimensions of war are *a priori* obvious. Wars happen somewhere – even cyberwars: despite the fact that attacks take place in a virtual space, repercussions are on concrete spaces of human activity and take place during a time period. The fact that war takes root in these two dimensions is irreducible, even if the range of these dimensions can vary greatly; indeed, a war can be more or less protracted, and it can take place in a small or a large area. Notions of both space and time together give to war a dimensionality, because it makes it able to change and to be multiple. The purpose here is not to use the scientific notion of space-time,[82] but to point out the fact that war is not a simple picture, object, or immutable event. Moreover, the mere process of defining something as a war consists in giving a single name and meaning to a complex sequence of realities. *De facto*, this definition mechanism reduces the plurality and makes it manageable. Although it is understandable, the internal complexity and diversity of war must not be forgotten. It is essential to stress that war first and foremost happens in space and during time – this is what gives war its plurality.

Michel Foucault points out notions of both space and time in his conception of war. In *Society Must Be Defended*, he argues that war is a matrix for power relations, it is a "point of maximum tensions."[83] Thereby, according to him, war is above all a time and a space structure in which men use techniques of

---

[82] Hermann Minkowski, within the context of his research on the special theory of relativity, was one of the first to develop the notion of "space-time," or "spacetime," combining the three spatial dimensions with that of time.
[83] Foucault, *Society*, 46.

domination in a global play for power. Foucault considers that society is entirely made up of power relations and that no spaces are protected from these domination struggles. "Power is not something that is divided between those who have it and hold it exclusively, and those who do not have it and are subject to it;"[84] power rather circulates and passes through individuals without being applied to them. Thereby, war is only a moment and a place in which power relations are at work and pass through. So, Foucault underlines the dimensionality of war because he primarily focuses on war as an expression and a carrier.

These space and time notions appear to be especially important and useful to understanding contemporary forms of warfare. This is supported by the statements of Münkler, who argues that the course of new wars is determined by the dispersion of forces in space and time. "Typically, then, the new wars lack what characterized the inter-state wars: the decisive battle which, for Clausewitz, was the 'real centre of gravity of the War.'"[85] The Second Congo War is one of these situations in which the space and time dimensions are confusing because they are fragmented, but at the same time they are essential in order to understand the conflict. In a different way, the temporal dimension has been essential in making the Vietnam War what it is. The evolution and outcomes of this conflict cannot be understood without the time dimension. These two wars will be analyzed in more detail in Part III.

Contemporary threats and corollary solutions break the precise distinction between war and peace. As Frédéric Gros suggests, in contemporary times we have moved from wars to states of violence (*états de violence*). This confusion of what constitutes war is typically exemplified by current threats (Islamic terrorism in the western countries, international criminality, or guerrilla warfare) and interventions (UN peacekeeping and assistance missions, preventive interventions, targeted airstrikes, special forces, or clandestine operations in

---

[84] *Ibid.*, 28.
[85] Münkler, The *New Wars*, 12.

non-war-zones). In these cases, war is not clearly defined in terms of time and space, war is not officially declared, there is a fluctuation of more or less violent moments, the civilian zone and the front are intermingled, operations take place far from the country being defended, situations tend to resemble security issues rather than military classical and visible threats, answers are low-key, etc.

Thus, one can see how decisive the space and time dimensions are in defining the pattern of conflict, the type of war, or even in defining war itself. To focus solely on the intricate nature of war in these dimensions leads to limiting and blinding oneself in the understanding of the war phenomenon. War is a sequence, not a snapshot. It is the awareness that war is a space-time construct, or in other words is fully embedded in the space and time dimensions, which highlights the fact that war is in perpetual adjustment, and that war is not a single and uniform piece but is complex and can be multiple at all levels, from the tactical to the political.

A Social Process

We are social creatures. Cultures, social structures, ideas, and ideologies shape all dimensions of violence, both its expressions and repressions.[86]

– N. Scheper-Hughes and P. Bourgois

As well as through the notions of space and time, the dimensions of war are also apparent in terms of social interactions. War is a social phenomenon. The social component is of cardinal importance to the fact that war is generative, plural, mutating, uncertain, and complex.

---

[86] Nancy Scheper-Hughes and Philippe Bourgois, eds., *Violence in War and Peace: An Anthology* (Malden: Blackwell Publishing, 2004), 3.

Individuals, groups, and their interactions participate in the dimensionality of war.

War is a human activity because those who move, act, and fight in it are men, and they give it meaning. More than a human activity, it is a social phenomenon because it is related to the lives of groups and societies. Indeed, war is not an isolated activity; it is by essence relational. War is not a fight with oneself and for oneself; people fight together and against each other. "A conflict can only arise in the presence of someone else or some others," states Julien Freund.[87]

It is true that war is, on the one hand, antisocial because it negates and tends to break social relations. On the other hand, even disagreements are social relations because warring parties recognize each other and do something together; in some way or another, they interact with each other. The French sociologist Gaston Bouthoul suggests that war is the most significant form of socialization: "La guerre est la plus marquante de toutes les formes de passage concevables dans la vie sociale."[88] This means that through war, people interact together like nowhere else because the entire social body is at play within war.

As war is a social process, it experiences the various kinds of situations and mutations that mark social relations in a group's life. In *The Sociology of Conflict*,[89] Georg Simmel explores the sociological thickness of conflicts in general, and consequently of wars themselves. He points out that conflicts can have a sociological significance in two different ways. Firstly, it can be due to their consequences or accompaniments, because "[they] either produce or modify communities of interest, unifications, organizations." In other words, wars modify social structures. Secondly, the conflict itself can be a

---

[87] Julien Freund, *Sociologie du Conflit* (Paris: Presses Universitaires de France, 1983), 19.
[88] Gaston Bouthoul, *Le phénomène guerre* (Paris: Payot, 2006), 12.
[89] Georg Simmel, "The Sociology of Conflict," *The American Journal of Sociology* 9, no.4, 5, and 6 (1904).

form of socialization, *i.e.*, wars are places in which social relations are changed. Most of the time, these are intertwined.

For instance, war is a social process with regard to what it can stimulate in terms of social cohesion of the group. War requires a concentration of energies and forces. In a group, it urges people to forget their differences and internal issues, to show solidarity with each other, and to fight for a common purpose. Thus, war has a potential power for social cohesion. This is what Simmel argues in the following passage:

> The champion must 'pull himself together'; that is, all his energies must be concentrated upon a single point at once, in order that at any moment they may be exerted in the direction demanded. In peace he may allow himself more latitude; that is, he may indulge the individual energy and interests of his nature which may take courses in various directions and somewhat independently of each other. In times of attack and defence, however, the consequence of this indulgence would be a waste of energy through counter efforts of the different impulses, and a loss of time through the necessity of assembling and organizing them in each instance. In such cases, therefore, the whole man must assume the form of concentration as his essential line of battle and means of defence. Conduct formally the same is demanded in the like situation of the group.[90]

Like Simmel but from a different perspective, Frederic Gros[91] and Jean Bodin[92] defend the idea that war contributes to the cohesion of the group. But they argue that war contributes to social unity by purging the society from harmful and deviant people because thieves and criminals express their wickedness against the enemy rather than within society.

Also, war has at times been affiliated with feasts in regard to its agitation and unifying features, which exist

---

[90] Simmel, "Sociology of Conflict," 672-673.
[91] *cf.* Frédéric Gros, *Etats de violence*, 131-132.
[92] *cf.* Jean Bodin, *Six Books of the Commonwealth*, trans. M.J. Tooley (New York: Macmillan, 1955), book V, chapter 5.

together. Roger Callois[93] wrote that war, like a feast, constitutes an absolute phenomenon of collective tension and a group's reviving; both are paroxysms of society. War and feast break habits as well as the linearity of peoples' lives; "they indiscriminately ruin fear and placidity,"[94] and bring stirrings and solidarity.

In a different way, Olivier Roy[95] explains how war has been, traditionally in Afghanistan, a way to organize society. The conflict is understood as a violent relationship aiming to assess a power struggle, which allows the elaboration of a future compromise. This conception of war is integrated in the traditional structures of solidarity, and related to the exercise of authority and to the distribution of goods and violence. War is a bloody action, however it remains a relationship and it is oriented toward the balance of social life. For Roy, people fight intermittently in Afghanistan; they neither try to annihilate the enemy, nor to topple the government. "War continuously aims to establish an equilibrium."[96]

Also, during war, the military institution itself can have a profound social impact. "War by definition is a social activity resting upon some kind of organization," suggests Martin van Creveld.[97] In times of war, because one of the most mobilized institutions is the military, it tends to be especially powerful, important, numerous, and influential. Consequently, its social imprint comes to be substantial. By way of example, in many African conflicts, the military institution is a refuge for people in terms of structure and subsistence, although they did not deliberately join the military.

---

[93] Roger Callois, *L'Homme et le sacré* (Paris: Flammarion, 1988).
[94] *Ibid.*, 222-223.
[95] *cf.* Olivier Roy, "Afghanistan: la guerre comme facteur de passage au politique," *Revue française de science politique* 39, no.6 (1989), and "Afghanistan: les raisons d'un conflit interminable," *Cultures & Conflits* 1 (Winter 1990).
[96] Roy, "Afghanistan: les raisons d'un conflit interminable," 6.
[97] Creveld, *Transformation of War*, 157.

War in general and conscription in particular can also provide opportunities for young people. Children and youngsters from poor backgrounds and with limited educational and employment opportunities have the chance to become someone by joining, perhaps even to be a commander in control of people who may be older and/or more educated.[98]

Indeed, for many young people, war becomes a way of social integration because they find a group, they can acquire an identity, they earn money, and they can have power and be respected; paradoxically, they can also be forced, raped, abused, or threatened. The military proposes new identification models, and as Luca Jourdan points out in speaking about the youth enlistment in North Kivu (Democratic Republic of the Congo), violence is used as an attempt to face a deep disorientation and a reality that is hard to deal with. Jourdan also suggests that becoming a soldier "constitutes nowadays one of the rare alternatives to social marginalization, being an opportunity for social mobility."[99] Voluntarily or not, war allows them to join a form of social life.[100]

More widely, wars are often so involving that they shape, affect, and include entire societies and what surrounds them. Thereby, wars potentially bring social change not only where they happen, but also around themselves. Ariel Colonomos points this out, arguing that consequences and implications of a conflict are many, and spread out to a considerable number of peoples and societies both involved or not in the conflict.[101] By way of example, a war can stimulate the activity of a diaspora, which can then have social

---

[98] Kendra E. Dupuy and Krijn Peters, *War and Children* (Santa Barbara: Praeger Security International, 2010), 62.

[99] Luca Jourdan, "Being at War, Being Young: Violence and Youth in North Kivu," in *Conflict and Social Transformation in Eastern DR Congo*, ed. Koen Vlassenroot and Timothy Raeymaekers, (Ghent: Academia Press, 2004), 157-175.

[100] The child soldiers phenomenon can be considered as social bands not fully related to wars. However, wars give them a reason to exist and to maintain their activity.

[101] Colonomos, *Pari de la guerre*, 245.

repercussions on the country where that diaspora lives; war can create solidarity between a warring country and another not directly involved in the conflict. A war can provoke migration flows, which can have substantial social effects on a bordering country.

The social body is not stable, especially not in war, which is an intense moment of reorganization. As presented in this chapter, war generates many contradictory social effects at an individual level as well as at a group level. However, understanding war as a social process does not mean that war produces this or that specific effect in societies; on the contrary, it first and foremost means that war is a very dynamic social moment in itself and in what it generates. The Second Congo War perfectly illustrates this complex social dimension of the war phenomenon, as will be seen in Part III. Destructive of social orders and systems, this war also generated new social orders through the mutation of political, cultural, and economic systems.

War is social in multiple aspects. It is a social phenomenon in terms of what it produces. Indeed, war can induce the whole range of possible changes in the social body; it can thereby produce unity and disunity, and this can even happen together. The conflict is about social re-engineering. For instance, war can solidify in the short term the military and political institutions, which can unify the people, and at the same time war can generate a long-term and profound destabilization of the entire social body. Besides their social productiveness, wars are expressions of civilization, as Roger Callois states;[102] war is a way of existence of societies into which the nation's productive forces are turned towards tasks of destruction or protection against destruction. Thus, war is also a human and social activity in itself. Making war is social; in other words, war is a social phenomenon in its immediacy.

I have presented war in its time, space, and social dimensions. This comprehension is essential if one wants to get

---

[102] Roger Callois, *Bellone ou La Pente de la guerre* (Saint Clément de Rivière: Fata Morgana, 1994), 14.

out of the unifying and freezing conceptions of war, and to understand war as a CAS or as an uncertain and self-modifying social phenomenon. Only when keeping these dimensions in mind can one understand war as generative, uncertain, and multiple.

CHAPTER 4
A PRODUCTIVE PHENOMENON

The idea that war itself might be something that can explain, that has itself the power of bestowing meaning, is an idea foreign to all philosophies of history and so also to all the explanations of war we know.[103]

– Jan Patočka

All the features and dimensions of war described until now are constitutive elements of the understanding of war as productive. It must be said, first of all, that to comprehend war as productive is not to make a moral judgment or to deny its destructive power; it is merely to present the generative aspect of war without any judgment. The aim is not to oppose productive to destructive, because this differentiation is based on a kind of moral judgment, or at least on a bias. In both cases, a new array of elements is created; what changes is the way one perceives it. Thus, what matters here is not to judge consequences of war, but to globally understand how generative war can be. And this productivity of war must be comprehended as consequences and correlated to the notions of uncertainty and autonomy, which then allow us to understand how war can change war.

---

[103] Jan Patočka, *Heretical Essays in the Philosophy of History* (Chicago: Open Court, 1996), 120.

Uncertain, Autonomous, and Self-Modifying

Unpredictable

War is powerful and generates many changes. Desired or endured, it is normal to do everything in one's power to influence it and to make it follow one's interest. But although detailed, rational, and planned might be the strategy to manage the situation, war remains uncertain and uncontrollable – at least for men. There is an inclination to think about war in terms of "how to make it" or "how to deal with it;" so, the uncertainty of the phenomenon is sent backward. The notion of uncertainty is perceived as working against human actions and the control of things. It is hard to set up rules if everything is unstable. If war is about controlling and managing a situation, then uncertainty does not help.

The psychologist Albert Bandura explains that uncertainty is very disturbing in human activity, and that correlatively control is a central element. People consequently develop beliefs and a confidence about what they can do; Bandura calls it self-efficacy. In his words, self-efficacy is "people's beliefs about their capabilities to produce designated levels of performance that exercise influence over events that affect their lives."[104] In order to act, someone has to consider that his/her action will produce a result; if not, he/she will not act. Central to behavior is the belief in its efficacy. Thus, one can easily understand why war tends to be reduced and rationalized, and why its unpredictability is minimized.

However, it would be wrong to say that the uncertainty of war is always passed over in silence. Most of the famous military strategists state the contingency and unpredictability of what is happening throughout war. The widespread notion of "fog of war" reflects this perception that war is not a

---

[104] Albert Bandura, "Self-efficacy," *Encyclopedia of human behavior*, ed. V. S. Ramachaudran, vol.4 (New York: Academic Press, 1994), 71-81.

phenomenon where everything is predictable, clear, and easy to deal with.

> The great uncertainty of all data in war is a peculiar difficulty, because all action must, to a certain extent, be planned in a mere twilight, which in addition not infrequently – like the effect of a fog or moonshine – gives to things exaggerated dimensions and unnatural appearance.[105]

Clausewitz is one of the first to apply the term "fog of war." He points out very clearly the uncertainty of war.

> War is the province of chance. In no sphere of human activity is such a margin to be left for this intruder, because none is so much in constant contact with him on all sides. He increases the uncertainty of every circumstance, and deranges the course of events.[106]

Having said that, the uncertainty asserted is, in a way, an issue that must be overcome. So yes, war is openly uncertain for Clausewitz, but, as with fog, the important thing is to circumvent it.

> War is the province of uncertainty: three-fourths of those things upon which action in war must be calculated, are hidden more or less in the clouds of great uncertainty. Here, then, above all a fine and penetrating mind is called for, to grope out the truth by the tact of its judgment.[107]

As has already been explained in the part concerning Clausewitz, uncertainty is mainly relegated by him to the details of planning (in terms of tactics, operations, or eventually strategy), because all this must be encapsulated into a political

---

[105] Clausewitz, *On War*, 63.
[106] *Ibid.*, 36.
[107] *Ibid.*, 36.

plan. Consequently, the analysis of Thomas J. Czerwinski,[108] who considers that Clausewitz perceives war as a profoundly nonlinear phenomenon, must be nuanced. From a larger perspective, war is not really uncertain for Clausewitz. In the end, action and certainty overcome unpredictability.

In a different way, besides the over-rationalistic trend of modern times fed by the numerous and always increasing technological possibilities, some contemporary theorists consider this uncertainty of war.[109] In the book *Décider dans l'incertitude*,[110] the French General Vincent Desportes underlines this primary feature of war, specifically its innate randomness and nonlinearity.

> Throughout the history of war, neither the numerous organizational changes, the greatest technological advances, nor the 'revolutions in military matters'… have really changed the fundamental problem confronting all operational decision-makers and their command systems: the problem of the uncertainty that derives from the complex and interactive nature of war.[111]

This fluidity and uncertainty of war is an uncomfortable truth that many soldiers are currently aware of. However, it is not openly confessed, maybe because public opinion would not understand, because war would appear less legitimate, because many hidden interests are at play, or simply because war is not purely rational but made of inconstancies and driven by its own inertia. The Balkan, Afghanistan, and African conflicts are perfect examples, and people in the field know it; they constantly readjust their strategies according to these changing

---

[108] Thomas J. Czerwinski is a retired professor of information warfare and strategy at the National Defense University.
[109] Such as *War: Ends and Means*, by Angelo Codevilla and Paul Seabury; *The Transformation of War*, by Martin van Creveld, and *Décider dans l'incertitude*, by Vincent Desportes.
[110] Translated under the title: *Deciding in the Dark*.
[111] Vincent Desportes, *Décider dans l'incertitude*, 2nd ed. (Paris: Economica, 2007), 113.

situations in order to keep the advantage. Having said that, they remain soldiers, their job is above all to focus on the use of the military coercion tool; "qu'elles s'y préparent ou la conduisent, l'action est la finalité des armées."[112] Even if this is legitimate coming from a soldier, once again, uncertainty disappears behind action.

In contrast to these practically oriented approaches, it is argued here that war is from A to Z uncertain and unpredictable, and not only in terms of tactics or strategy, but in its socio-political aspects also. War is, in essence, a place in which everything interacts and gives a result that is not foreseeable. Even if one engages in a war for a specific reason, what happens in the course of war is not under control. No one can master all the consequences of his actions. As Julien Freund asserts when analyzing Max Weber's thought, actors must reappraise their positions, readjust their means, and sometimes postpone or even cancel their undertakings due to the unwilling effects, which threaten interests and ideals they were fighting for.[113]

When people look back *a posteriori* on a war, they find explanations, they draw conclusions, they find regularities, and they establish some behavioral patterns. However, the future in war is always much more unstable and unpredictable than people hope. As Nassim Nicholas Taleb, the philosopher of uncertainty, fairly points out, "we humans, facing limits of knowledge, and things we do not observe, the unseen and the unknown, resolve the tension by squeezing life and the world into crisp commoditized ideas."[114]

War is uncertain or unpredictable because it is a nonlinear phenomenon. In contrast to linear systems which imply "proportionality, additivity, replication, and

---

[112] *Ibid.*, 9.
[113] Julien Freund, *Max Weber* (Paris: Presses Universitaires de France, 1969), 31.
[114] Nassim Nicholas Taleb, *The Bed of Procrustes: Philosophical and Practical Aphorisms* (New York: Random House, 2010), xii.

demonstrability of causes and effects,"[115] and thus in which inputs and outputs are proportional, more precisely in which there is an understandable, defined, and clear relation between inputs and outputs, nonlinear systems are more sophisticated, and they consequently take directions that are not foreseeable. As Czerwinski explains, "nonlinear systems are those that disobey proportionality. They may exhibit erratic behavior through disproportionately large or disproportionately small outputs, or they may involve 'synergistic' interactions in which the whole is not equal to the sum of the parts."[116] This notion of nonlinearity goes hand in hand with the notions of complexity and adaptability that are presented in the following part concerning CAS.

The uncertainty of war and its consequences are subconsciously known by warring parties; people fight for reasons and defend their identities, and do that in order to try to impact the future in their ways and according to their will. It is because of this uncertainty of the future that war is done. Actually, as Colonomos argues, war is a gamble.[117] By definition, war is uncertain and theories are attempts to face this uncertainty. On the one hand, people and their theories try to master and forecast war, and on the other hand war is done because the future is not defined. In a sense, if the future were certain, wars would not be fought; thereby, war is purely an uncertain phenomenon.

---

[115] Thomas J. Czerwinski, *Coping with the Bounds: A Neo-Clausewitzean Primer*, revised ed. (Washington, DC: DoD Command and Control Research Program, 2008), 8.
[116] Alan Beyerchen, "Clausewitz, Nonlinearity and the Unpredictability of War," *International Security* 17, no.3 (Winter 1992), 64.
[117] Colonomos, *Pari de la Guerre*.

Autonomous and Self-Modifying

War 'smoulders on', 'spreads out', 'extends over' and so on.[118]
– Herfried Münkler

Ending war is, if anything, a problem more complex than war itself.[119]
– Matthew Moten

War is alive. War is very powerful because it generates substantial and uncontrollable series of causes and consequences; thereby, war tends to develop a certain degree of autonomy. Because war is not a snapshot but a sequence happening in time and space, it creates new logics as it advances. In the course of action, even systems of reference change; in other words, not only the action and the context are mutating, but also the way to interpret them alters. As war moves forward, perceptions, minds, and ideas mutate. Consequently, politics, strategy, and tactics are changing throughout war. These changes and readjustments are inherent to war; it makes war what it is – a very serious, risky, and unpredictable game that each actor tries to win.

Wars become systems producing meaning, identity, structure, and profit; and the wider and longer the war, the more likely this is to happen. Having assumed autonomy, war expands its self-guidance and evolves into something new; this is why war is self-modifying. To be precise, war cannot become entirely autonomous, but it is called autonomous because as soon as a war begins, it loses its subordination to the men who

---

[118] Münkler, The *New Wars*, 33-34.
[119] Matthew Moten, ed., *Between War and Peace: How America Ends its Wars* (New York: Free Press, 2011), x.

started it. War is animated by its own life, as General Desportes[120] writes.

All conflicts mutate through time: they are not static. They stop, stagnate, and widen. On the one hand, war is rooted in the past, and is consequently subject to its inertia. On the other hand, things are not immutable and clearly defined. War modifies and adds elements to the "matrix," which shapes the future.

A war can start for a reason and continue for another one, as can be seen, for example, in the US-NATO Afghan War, from 2001 to the present. A domestic conflict can become a regional war, as in the Democratic Republic of the Congo, from 1998 to 2003. A "terrorist" group can become a legitimate political group during the course of a conflict. Ideological reasons and economic interests can interchange repeatedly as the leading purpose of a conflict.

Based on a few examples – the Seven Years' War, the French Revolutionary and Napoleonic Wars, the Crimean War, World War One – Stacy Bergstrom Haldi develops a "war widening theory" focusing on interstate wars. According to Haldi, what determines war widening is the political cost of warfare, which in turn causes predation and balancing.

> When the political cost of warfare is low – that is, when states are in little danger of being destroyed – they are more likely to join other states' conflicts as predatory opportunities present themselves. Conversely, when the political cost of warfare is high – that is, when war entails the risk of annihilation – states are less likely to join wars for predatory reasons, but will join them for balancing reasons.[121]

---

[120] Vincent Desportes, *Comprendre la guerre*, 2nd ed. (Paris: Economica, 2001), 351.
[121] Stacy Bergstrom Haldi, *Why Wars Widen: A Theory of Predation and Balancing* (London: Frank Cass, 2003), 158.

In *Les Guerres en chaîne,* Raymond Aron also emphasizes how war is not fixed but changing, developing its own logics and rhythms. According to Aron, battles transform the initial motives of war, most particularly in the twentieth century. War is hyperbolic, "tout se passe comme si, à partir d'un certain degrès, la violence s'entretenait elle-même."[122] War is not about a unique cause or consequence effect, it is rather about a series of reactions packed with inconsistencies fascinating observers – the gap between causes and effects, the gap between ideological and power conflicts and the true stakes of these conflicts, the gap between passions of men and the consequence of their actions.[123]

Globally, war tends to develop its own logic and independence. Clausewitz dreaded this development, which is why he wished to keep war under the control of politics. Even if this remains desirable, such subordination of war to politics is impossible because war is a living phenomenon, it is action in process, and it necessarily changes its colors as it unfolds. This is not to say that dogs of war should be released without any care for politics, nor that the carnage of war is acceptable. Rather, war as politics is in perpetual readjustment and interaction. Clausewitz confined war to politics, and as a result it is reduced to something fixed that emanates from a state. And yet, in practice, war is precisely the human phenomenon that cannot be mastered.

In contrast to Clausewitz's perspective, Creveld points out how war can be separated from its beginning. Firstly, war can change; men can start to fight for a reason, but nothing guarantees that they will continue to fight for the same reason, especially if the conflict lasts.[124] Secondly, war has something immediate which makes it constantly move away from the past. So far from any plans, there is the immediacy of war. In other words, war comes to be about survival and self-defense. Forecasts or specific aims disappear behind the simple struggle

---

[122] Aron, *Guerres en chaîne,* 36.
[123] *Ibid.,* 112.
[124] Creveld, *Transformation of War,* 188.

for life. "War not merely serves power, it is power."[125] Following these lines, Creveld breaks the logic of the clear distinction between ends and means, and of the way to think about war as a tool serving specific interests. Sometimes, war is profitable to nobody and has no particular purpose; it is a mere expression of life. Creveld even argues that almost all wars tend to become like that; such was the case for World War I and World War II.

> Our analysis...has taken for granted the Clausewitzian distinction between war, the means, and whatever its ends might be. Over history, the ends for which people have fought have been extremely diverse. They have included every kind of secular "interest," such as territorial expansion, power, and profit; but they have also compromised abstract ideals such as law, justice, "rights," and the greater glory of God, all served in various combinations with each other and the secular interests. While the above criteria are useful up to a point, paradoxically they leave out what is perhaps the most important single form of war in all ages. This, of course, is war for the community's existence.[126]

Following these lines, the Czech philosopher Jan Patočka gives a penetrating insight by exploring how war can be an end rather than a means to an end. According to Patočka, war is the most efficient and quick way to release the energy and the power stored.[127] He uses the experience of the front-line to penetrate the inside of war and its autonomous meaning. The brute experience of the front-line action – mixing absurdity, inconsistency, brutality, and freedom – shakes humans and transforms them. By describing freedom, Patočka shows how the forthright experience of war becomes an end in itself, and thus purely autonomous. Patočka's view, which seems to correspond to First World War kinds of assaults, still makes sense for many African conflicts, or more widely to understand

---

[125] *Ibid.*, 219.
[126] Creveld, *Transformation of War*, 142.
[127] Patočka, *Heretical Essays*, 129-132.

some release of violence in contemporary conflicts. Even in western armies, this kind of behavior remains conceivable, as was the case during the Iraq or Afghanistan wars. Soldiers are not pure rational machines that faithfully personify the political will. They are human, complex, and changing, and also have their own logics and issues interfering with their mission.

> (T)he participants are assaulted by *an absolute freedom*, freedom from *all* the interests of peace, of life, of the day. That means: the sacrifice of the sacrificed loses its relative significance, it is no longer the cost we pay for a program of development, progress, intensification, and extension of life's possibilities, rather, it is significant *solely in itself*.[128]

Creveld and Patočka are right to describe war in an anti-teleogical way. However, things are rather mixed up. War's ways exceed its initial purpose, if there is one. Neither only a means nor only an end, a war is in practice alternating between both; more so, war is both a tool and an end.

That said, due to the fact that war is an expression of society, each society makes, uses, and lives war in a different way. Each civilization articulates differently its meaning and its making of war. Its culture, structures, myths, ideologies, organization, institutions, and political system make it apprehend war in a specific way; thereby, war is sometimes more a means, sometimes more an end. Currently, in most western states, the political reasoning and the state try to organize war and to keep it under control by making it out to be only a means. However, this does not prevent it from remaining autonomous, evolving, self-modifying, and very different from what it had been started for. War develops its own logics, which makes it much more than a mere tool. Obviously, this is even more the case when warring parties are non-state actors. The wars examined in Part III are examples of this.

War is not a moving ball, autonomous from everything. War progressively turns away from its beginning, which is why

---

[128] *Ibid.*, 129-130.

it is considered as autonomous; but war constantly creates new connections because it is embedded in all dimensions of life. This is how war is self-modifying. War is always a mix of ends and means, because it is actually the destiny of all human actions. War is in motion, it always serves new purposes, destroys past ones, and creates new ones.

War and Politics: A Dialectical Approach

Politics acts on war as much as war acts on politics. Exploring the link between war and politics is especially important in our times, because the international system – *i.e.*, international law, institutions, and organizations – and most states consider war purely as a political tool, war being the *ultima ratio* used to defend the sovereignty of a country. And there is the constant will to make war fit this pattern. However, in practice, war does not follow this ideal paradigm. The relationship between these two notions is less linear and simple than what is globally admitted, and rightly so because war is autonomous, productive, and complex. The purpose here is to show how politics can mutate, be destructed or created throughout war. In other words, what matters here is to understand how war, throughout its own course and not *a posteriori*, is generative of political changes. A few brief examples will be exposed in this section, while more detailed analyses of the mutations of politics in war will be seen in the cases described in Part III.

Clausewitz's statement, which says that war is merely a continuation of politics by other means, can be considered as incorrect for four main reasons. Firstly, the contemporary perception of war as a "terrible" but necessary tool following a state policy/reason is based on a specific cultural pattern, which is neither universal nor eternal. In other words, war will very likely have other meanings and uses in the future. Secondly, war and politics are in a mutually shaping process. Accordingly, they both change as war progresses. Thirdly, in contemporary conflicts, warring parties are more erratic than the kind of organized groups on which Clausewitz based his reasoning. Fourthly, when states are at war, the state machine itself can also forget its reasonable and coherent political reason. As Roger Callois[129] argues, the heavy machine, which serves man, enslaves him by serving him. Men are no longer combatants, they are slaves and victims of this state, and thus of war.

For instance, in *Afghanistan: La guerre comme facteur du passage au politique*, Olivier Roy shows how war and politicization work together. It is the militarization that enables a group to become a political actor. Roy explains that, for the various Afghan leaders, the first priority is not to build a centralized state, it is rather to keep local powers. Thus, following the traditional models of war in Afghanistan, war allows one to stay in this in-between state; specifically, war balances society by creating and destroying political legitimacies.

Focusing on Afghanistan too, Antonio Giustozzi explores the notion of warlordism and its place in the state and political formation. Through *Empires of Mud: Wars and Warlords in Afghanistan*, Giustozzi argues that if warlords stick to their military origins and build nothing durable, they do not participate in state formation. But in practice, they tend to participate in "processes of cross-fertilization conductive to state formation."[130] Following these lines, Giustozzi presents in another text[131] the genesis of the "Prince" Ismail Khan, who used war to institutionalize and legitimize himself in political terms. So, warlords are not only military commanders running for themselves in war, they also tend to politicize their power.

---

[129] Callois, *Bellone*, 225-234.
[130] Antonio Giustozzi, *Empires of Mud: Wars and Warlords in Afghanistan* (New York: Columbia University Press, 2009), 2.
[131] Antonio Giustozzi, "Genesis of a 'Prince': The Rise of Ismail Khan in Western Afghanistan, 1979-1992," *Crisis State Working Papers*, no.4 (2006).

In the same way, William Reno[132] explores warlordism in Africa. He raises similar conclusions by underlining the fact that warlords are not only private entrepreneurs running for their own interests, but they also tend to develop socio-political roles in terms of organization, regulation, or protection.[133]

Also focusing on Africa, Koen Vlassenroot and Timothy Raeymaekers take the example of the Democratic Republic of the Congo to show the production of new political orders in war.

> In most conflict regions, however, the decrease in the competence of the state and the formation of rebel movements and militias...have given leeway to the formation of new, non-state centres of authority that have in turn introduced new modes of political, social and economic control. Contrary to the dominant discourse that war-torn societies find themselves caught in a conflict-trap, most conflicts tend to produce new orders out of anarchy and destruction. Although these new orders are almost invariably violent, exploitative, and illiberal in character, these are "orders, not anarchy," and their development sometimes constitutes the best chance for a country or community to emerge into something worthy of the expression of "post-conflict."[134]

They argue that the new orders developed along the conflict are characterized by new processes of local elite accommodation and adaptation, as well as by different patterns of socio-economic interactions between elites, non-state armed

---

[132] See his following works: *Warlord Politics and African States* (Boulder: Rienner, 1998); "The Changing Nature of Warfare and the Absence of State-Building in West Africa," in *Irregular Armed Forces and their Role in Politics and State Formation* (Cambridge: Cambridge University Press, 2004).

[133] In the same way, see Münkler, *The New Wars*, 91. The figure of the warlord is defined as a combination of entrepreneurial, political, and military logic in a single person.

[134] Vlassenroot and Raeymaekers, *Formation of Centres of Profit, Power, and Protection*, 1.

actors, and grassroots populations. David J. Francis, through the notion of civil militia, equally shows how socio-political structures become transformed in wars. The birth of civil militia in wars demonstrates that civil society is far from disintegrating, and shows in contrast a great resilience in providing public goods for the community and necessities for existence. In many contemporary sub-Saharan conflicts, however destructive and deadly wars are, they paradoxically propose new political orders, as has been the case in the Democratic Republic of the Congo.[135] Wars are in-motion processes; the society restructures itself in the dimensions of war.

Some authors have already exposed how war can be generative of politics, but in such ways that the dimensions of war and the dialectical relationship between war and politics are not presented. Charles Tilly[136] and Eiko Ikegami[137] explain how war can contribute to state formation, and consequently how war can generate political structures and thoughts. However, they reversed Clausewitz's idea by placing war before politics. Although their demonstration is coherent, it opens the infinite debate of "which came first, the chicken or the egg?" and it consequently remains stuck in a simplifying cause-consequence pattern. With their approach, one can understand the productivity of war but not its dimensions. The focus is put on post-war effects, whereas ours is to focus on war itself.

---

[135] Explained in detail in Part III.
[136] Tilly reversed Clausewitz's assertion by demonstrating that European state-making ensued from war making. In the article "War Making and State Making as Organized Crime," he explains the place of organized means of violence in the growth and change of national states. Tilly aims to point out the interdependence of war-making and the construction of the European states until the nineteenth century; "war makes states."
[137] Ikegami, in "Military Mobilization and the Transformation of Property Relationships: Wars That Defined the Japanese Style of Capitalism," shows how war-making contributed to state and cultural formation in Japan. She explains the various political transformations that resulted from war.

Foucault[138] proposes an alternative view. For him, everything starts with war, which is the motor of institutions, order, and exercise of political power. War is like the pure expression of power struggles, being comparable to the heart and the beginning of all human and political relationships. On the one hand, his holistic view – global perspective on power in society rather than a focus on the war phenomenon – is convincing because it seems more complete. On the other hand, it is more generalizing, and thus less useful to grasping the internal aspects of war.

In contrast to these authors and with regard to the examples previously given, it is argued here that neither war nor politics are fixed. War and politics are built simultaneously. These are two human activities, and both move, mutate, and interact with each other. On the one hand, politics tries to lead war and make it follow its strategy. On the other hand, war generates changes in the political framework. In other words, war is neither a continuation of politics, nor is politics a mere continuation of war; war is a mix and a complex sequence of interactions that changes the forms of politics, and of war itself.

That said, it must not be forgotten that what people call politics is only one of the many motivations of war, as could be

---

[138] Like Tilly, Foucault inverts Clausewitz's quote by saying that "politics is a continuation of war." Foucault considers that politics constitutes a transfer and a different expression of forces in action in war. The role of political power is thus to reinscribe this power struggle through institutions, economic inequalities, language, and individuals. "Politics, in other words, sanctions and reproduces the disequilibrium of forces manifested in war."
Consequently, peace is equivalent to a silent war for Foucault. Actually, war, struggles, and the clashes between forces are both principle and motor of the exercise of political power. Everything starts with war, which is the motor of institutions and order. So, for instance, law is not peace; on the contrary, it is the continuation of war but in a more institutionalized and organized way. In Foucault's thought, the limit between war and peace becomes blurred, the notion of politics becomes very wide, and war loses its specificity. Power is everywhere, and drives human relations in war as well as in peace. War is the initial energy, pushing and stimulating the entire society. War is like the pure expression of power struggles, comparable to the heart and the beginning of all human and political relationships.

money or ideals, such as human rights. As previously stated, these different motivations are mixed and interact constantly with each other throughout war. Moreover, the very conception of "interests" is insufficient to explain the making of war. It hides an overconfidence in the rationality and predictability of men and war; it remains stuck to a teleogical pattern. In this manner, Creveld rightly underlines that "the contemporary strategic premise that sees wars as making sense only when they are fought for reasons of policy or interest represents a point of view that is both Eurocentric and modern."[139]

---

[139] Creveld, *Transformation of War*, 155.

CHAPTER 5
UNDERSTANDING WAR AS A COMPLEX ADAPTIVE SYSTEM

Being nonlinear, autonomous, and self-modifying, it has been shown how war is generative, and among other things how it can be generative of politics. War destroys, creates, and changes what is tied to it as well as its own properties. It is this perspective on war as a complex auto-modifying phenomenon that this chapter seeks to explain through the very notion of CAS.

The Notion of Complexity

The first question to be answered is, What is complexity? Ironically, "there is no rigorous definition of complexity,"[140] as Neil Johnson states. That said, the hidden meaning behind the notion must be understood. A good start is Johnson's description, "Complexity Science can be seen as the study of the phenomena which emerge from a collection of interacting objects."[141]

Epistemologically, the word comes from the Latin *complexus*, which means "what is woven together." The French sociologist Edgar Morin,[142] who spent his entire career studying the notion of complexity, defined it as a set of heterogeneous components inseparably tied; "it is the paradox of the single and

---

[140] Johnson, *Simply Complexity*, 13.
[141] *Ibid.*, 3-4.
[142] Edgar Morin, "Restricted Complexity, General Complexity," trans. Carlos Gershenson. (paper presented at the colloquium *Intelligence de la complexité: épistémologie et pragmatique*, Cerisy-La-Salle, France, June 26, 2005).

the multiple."[143] In physics, complexity is the degree of the self-organization of a system.[144]

Complex is different from complicated. "A complex system dies when an element is removed, but complicated ones continue to live on, albeit slightly compromised."[145] In other words, complication expresses a high level of interconnectivity and of exchange, but the system remains linear. By contrast, when a system is complex, the interdependence and interconnectedness is much more elaborate; but what especially matters is the fact that a complex system is nonlinear, which is tied to the notion of emergence.[146] As Alan D. Beyerchen explains, "the heart of the matter is that the system's variables cannot be effectively isolated from each other or from their context; linearization is not possible, because dynamic interaction is one of the system's defining characteristics."[147]

Complex Adaptive System

War is a CAS, being a system that has a large number of components that interact and adapt or learn. A system is a set of interacting elements forming an integrated whole; the entire system displays properties that are different from those of the separate parts. If the interactions between the elements of the system as well as their behavior are not linear, nor proportional,

---

[143] Morin, *Complexité humaine*, 316.
[144] *A Dictionary of Physics*, ed. John Daintith, Oxford Reference Online (New York: Oxford University Press, 2009), *s.v.* "complexity."
[145] John H. Miller and Scott E. Page, *Complex Adaptive Systems: An Introduction to Computational Models of Social Life* (Princeton: Princeton University Press, 2007), 9.
[146] By emergence, I refer to the definition of Jeffrey Goldstein: "the arising of novel and coherent structures, patterns and properties during the process of self-organization in complex systems" (*Emergence: A Journal of Complexity Issues in Organizations and Management* 1, no.1 (1999), 49-72). Goldstein considers that the common characteristics of emergence are radical novelty; coherence or correlation; a global or macro level; dynamical; ostensive.
[147] Alan Beyerchen, "Clausewitz, Nonlinearity and the Unpredictability of War," *International Security* 17, no.3 (Winter 1992), 69.

and somehow random, the system can be considered as complex. The complex system becomes adaptive when the entities of the system adapt; in other words, when the rules of this system change.

In *Simply Complexity: A Clear Guide to Complexity Theory*,[148] Johnson identifies eight features characterizing a complex system. These features will now be addressed in turn, and their relevance reviewed.

The system contains a collection of many interacting objects or "agents." This applies to war, which is, in essence, an interplay of agents and objects – individuals, groups, countries, companies, organizations, weapon systems, and events.

These objects' behavior is affected by memory or "feedback." This means that something from the past affects something in the present, or that something going on at one location affects what is happening at another. The time dimension of war, previously discussed, automatically implies the notions of feedback and memory.

The objects can adapt their strategies according to their history. Things are not fixed in war; in contrast, they are deeply impacted by what happened before. Knowing that agents are human beings or groups, they evolve throughout time and constantly adapt to the situation. Thus, each agent has its own trajectory, which is marked by an evaluative strategy.

The system is typically "open." This means that the system can be influenced by its environment. Wars are never closed; they are always in contact with a specific environment. For instance, the international legal system, the financial market, the internal political situation of the country, the international community, or the regional political situation can be considered as environments, and they obviously impact wars.

---

[148] Johnson, *Simply Complexity*, 13-15.

The system appears to be "alive." The system evolves in a highly non-trivial and often complicated way, driven by an ecology of agents that interact and adapt under the influence of feedback. In war, things are not fixed and organized; they are interacting and mutating. War is somewhat alive because it is made up of a set of interacting agents, themselves alive and changing.

The system exhibits emergent phenomena, which are generally surprising, and may be extreme. This is one of the main principles of war. Clausewitz clearly described it through the notion of friction. The outcomes of war are emergent, expressly they are the unforeseen and non-proportional result of the interaction of numerous variables.

The emergent phenomena typically arise in the absence of any sort of "invisible hand" or central controller. This goes with the previous feature, and it is consequently the case for war. Things are not organized and fixed by one political will that would be considered an invisible hand. Emergence and generativeness of war are incompatible with any sort of invisible hand.

The system shows a complicated mix of ordered and disordered behavior. If a soldier or anybody on the battlefield were asked, they would tell this truism. Even the strategists and politicians are aware of this mix between order and disorder, but they do not claim this excessively because their job is to control the situation.

Thus, war can be considered a complex system. But it must be added that, in war, the agents and the system are adaptive because the individual and collective behaviors of its agents change as a result of experience, and that can affect war itself. In other words, war is like an "ecosystem," given that central to the ecosystem concept is the idea that living organisms are continually engaged in a set of relationships with every other element constituting the environment in which they exist. For instance, the arrival of a new weapon system or the change in warring parties' interests affects the war system. Hence, war is a CAS.

However scientific CAS sounds, it echoes some classical and old philosophical thoughts, such as the notion of circularity, flows, and interconnectivity. Heraclitus underlined these concepts a long time ago.

> The death of fire is birth for air, and the death of air is birth for water.[149]
>
> The beginning and the end are shared in the circumference of a circle.[150]
>
> They do not comprehend how a thing agrees at variance with itself; it is an attunement turning back on itself, like that of the bow and the lyre.[151]
>
> War is father of all and king of all.[152]
>
> Graspings: wholes and not wholes, convergent divergent, consonant, dissonant, from all things one and from one thing all.[153]

Thus, applying the notion of CAS to war recycles some interesting philosophical notions, and synthesizes them into one easily grasped concept. Accordingly, it can appear to be an easy way to define and grasp what is not understood, in other words a manner to hide our ignorance of war mechanisms. As the scientist Henry Atlan[154] says, complexity is the measure of our ignorance. On the contrary, CAS is a model that "allows us to explore the space between equilibrium and chaos;"[155] it makes possible the underlining of some essential features of war.

Beyond the theoretical and conceptual aspects of understanding war as a CAS, it has concrete implications. One of them is that it exposes how western democratic states are challenged by contemporary conflicts. Their fluidity is very

---

[149] Heraclitus, *Fragments*, 47.
[150] *Ibid.*, 75.
[151] *Ibid.*, 65.
[152] *Ibid.*, 67.
[153] *Ibid.*, 85.
[154] Henri Atlan, "L'intuition du complexe et ses théorisations," in *Les théories de la complexité, Autour de l'œuvre d'Henri Atlan* (Paris: Seuil, 1991), 9-42.
[155] Miller and Page, *Complex Adaptive Systems*, 220.

hard to apprehend for these very rigid, centralized, bureaucratic, and slow-reacting modern states. This is why the notion of CAS is a useful way for contemporary strategic and political thinking to introspect and reinvent itself.

PART III

THE SECOND CONGO WAR AND THE US-VIETNAM WAR

INTRODUCTION

The focus now will be on the Second Congo War (1998-2003) and the Vietnam War until the end of US involvement (1954-1973) to see how war is a CAS. Congo is a good case, being a typical example of contemporary developing world conflicts which break classical conceptualizations of war. It is a very complex, multi-faceted, and fluid conflict. It mixes local, regional, and international issues, while economics, ideology, politics, and ethnicity interacted together as pretexts for war. The Vietnam War is a different kind, which is *a priori* more linear and simpler, notably because it is more state-centric and embedded in the Cold War pattern. However, even in such a conflict, complexity is in action also.

These two examples are not the very picture of all wars, they are only *ideal types*. They have been chosen because they represent two extremes; one seems fluid, not centralized, and nonlinear, whereas the other one seems fixed, linear, and clear. However limited the understanding of the chain of interactions in war might be, both will show that a conflict can start for a reason, continue for another one, and end for yet a different one. The trajectory of an actor in war[156] is nonlinear. In other words, it will underline that war is a CAS – expressly, it is a process in motion.

---

[156] "Trajectory" must be understood as the social, political, and strategic lines followed by actors. Indeed, actors (individuals or groups) do not have fixed strategic or political positions; these change. This is why the term "trajectory" is used.

CHAPTER 6
THE SECOND CONGO WAR (1998-2003)

Coalitions started to shift almost overnight in a spectacular fashion.[157]
– Filip Reyntjens

The Second Congo War started in 1998 and officially ended in 2003. However, the reality is more nuanced in terms of timing. This war is actually the continuation of the First Congo War, which started in 1996, and which was itself the outcome of national and regional instabilities. With regard to how it ended, negotiations took place in late 2002 and led to an agreement signed in December of the same year, which was formally ratified by all the parties in April 2003. However, tensions and violence continued and still persist, especially in the Kivus.

Citizens are still confronted with an extortion of their economic activity, the imposition of forced taxes, summary killings, detentions, and executions, as well as systematic sexual violence against women and girls. Even as Congo moves toward greater political and economic stability, the "smoldering" conflict that has ruled people's lives for years continues to determine the living conditions of large parts of the rural areas in the eastern sections of the country.[158]

---

[157] Filip Reyntjens, "Briefing: The Second Congo War: More Than a Remake," *African Affairs* 98, no.391 (1999), 247.
[158] R. Beneduce, L. Jourdan, T. Raeymaekers, and K. Vlassenroot, "Violence with a purpose: exploring the functions and meaning of violence in the Democratic Republic of Congo," *Intervention: International Journal of Mental Health, Psychosocial Work and Counseling in Areas of Armed Conflict* 4, no.1 (2006), 32.

In the background, the Democratic Republic of the Congo (DRC) was experiencing different troubles: structural weaknesses (in terms of economy, administration, and politics), land issues, national and identity tensions, the emergence of a new political context (the end of Mobutu Sese Seko and the arrival of Laurent-Désiré Kabila), and tensions with neighboring countries (mainly Rwanda and Uganda). It is in this global framework that the conflict started.

In order to grasp the variations of the purposes of the war, this part will commence by presenting the actors' evolution. Then it will show how the war developed its own dynamics, becoming a system in itself. From there, it will be possible to better grasp the mutations in reasons to fight as the war proceeded, and thus to understand this conflict as a CAS.

Actors' Trajectories and Interactions

Throughout the war, the actors were numerous and changing, and their trajectories were not stable. Countries, rebel groups, militias, and leaders were fluid entities. They changed, were created, merged, and disappeared. Entries and exits were multiple; they marked the life of the conflict.[159] Although it is harder to build a unique and comprehensive approach, especially in the world's twelfth biggest country as it experienced numerous issues mixing and cumulating with each other, this complex set resulted in an outcome called the Second Congo War. The analysis of some actors and their trajectories in the following paragraphs helps us understand the complexity and the fluctuation of the purpose of war.

Ten countries were more or less directly involved: Angola, Burundi, Chad, the Democratic Republic of the Congo,

---

[159] I apologize in advance if I do not mention some small groups and if I simplify a bit the identities and evolutions of the ones discussed; this is to favor a clearer understanding of the main themes, as presenting every detail would have made it an indescribable mess.

Libya, Namibia, Rwanda, Sudan, Uganda, and Zimbabwe. Furthermore, around thirty rebel groups and militias were engaged.[160]

At the beginning of the war, the Congolese president (Kabila) decided to distance himself from his former allies (Rwanda and Uganda). As a result, tensions increased. Rather than withdrawing its troops from the eastern parts of Congo where they were stationed, Rwanda increased its presence in Goma and Bukavu. From then on, Rwanda allied with Uganda, and Burundi entered the conflict. They engaged in the hostilities directly, by helping other groups such as Banyamulenge militias.

On the other side, Kabila was backed by different countries. Angola, preoccupied by its own domestic stability and security, was concerned about the ties linking UNITA (an Angolan anti-governmental group) and the Congolese rebels. Consequently, Angola sent thousands of soldiers to help Kabila. Zimbabwe did the same, however the reasons for its involvement were diverse. Economic ties between the two countries were important, and Congo owed a crucial debt to

---

[160] Alliance of Democratic Forces for the Liberation of Congo (AFDL, Rwanda-Uganda backed alliance), Allied Democratic Forces (ADF), Army for the Liberation of Rwanda (ALiR), Banyamulenge,[160] Congolese Popular Army (CPA/APC), Democratic Forces for the Liberation of Rwanda (FDLR), Front de Libération du Congo (FLC), Interahamwe,[160] Katanga Tigers, Lord's Resistance Army (LRA), Maï-Maï,[160] groups (Bulenda Padir's group, Lwengamia Dunia's group, Forces Unies de Résistance Nationale contre l'Agression de la République Démocratique du Congo – FURNAC, Mouvement de Lutte contre l'Agression au Zaïre – MLAZ, Front de Résistance et de Défense du Kivu – FRDKI, Mudundu 40, etc.), Movement for the Liberation of Congo (MLC), National Council for the Defense of Democracy – Forces for the Defense of Democracy (CNDD-FDD), National Council for the Defense of Democracy – Forces for the Defense of Democracy (CNDD-FDD), National Liberation Front (FLN/FROLINA), National Union for Total Independence of Angola (UNITA), Nationalist and Integrationist Front (FNI), Rally for Congolese Democracy (RCD), Rassemblement Démocratique pour le Rwanda (RDR), RCD-Congo (faction of RCD-Goma), RCD-Goma, RCD-Kisangani (RCD-K/ML or RCD-Wamba), Sudan People's Liberation Army/Movement (SPLA/M), Union of Congolese Patriots (UPC).

Zimbabwe. Namibia equally responded positively to help Kinshasa by sending hundreds of men. Namibia's interests were less obvious, although it seems that economics was a key aspect, notably diamonds in Western Kasai. By the end of September 1998, Sudan, Chad, and Libya had also entered the conflict more or less directly. Sudan, which previously supported Mobutu's regime against Kabila's rebellion, now supported Kabila in this war; the reason being that Khartoum was strongly opposed to Uganda. Chad agreed to intervene mainly in order to regain influence in the region. Libya was not particularly close to Kabila's regime, but backed him for economic reasons, to regain influence, and to break its international isolation imposed by the United Nations.

Numerous armed groups participated in the conflict. They were tied to, backed, and used by the various powers involved. Their trajectories were even more complex and evolving than those of the countries.

Various leaders who broke away from Kabila's government (such as Jean-Pierre Bemba, Nande Mbusa Nyamwisi, Jean-Baptiste Tibasima, and Roger Lumbala) moved to Kivu, Ituri, and Orientale in order to join rebel groups. They became kinds of warlords, having varied and changing agendas.

Elsewhere, the conflict was hiding ethnic facets in some areas, such as among the Hema, Lendu, and Ngiti populations in Ituri.

In the Kivu, there were the Maï-Maï. As Jean-Claude Willame explains, Maï-Maï were made up of numerous groups who were undisciplined, unorganized, and uncoordinated; their leaders' agendas were confused, being a mix of economic, political, and ethnic logics.[161] On the whole, Maï-Maï were aligned to Kabila in the context of an "anti-Tutsi" coalition.[162]

---

[161] Jean-Claude Willame, *La Guerre du Kivu: Vues de la salle climatisée et de la véranda* (Brussels: Editions GRIP, 2010), 54.
[162] For more information, see Filip Reyntjens, *The Great African War: Congo and Regional Geopolitics, 1996-2006* (New York: Cambridge University Press, 2009), 203.

Another rebel group called the Congolese Rally for Democracy (known as RCD – Rassemblement Congolais pour la Démocratie), which fought against Kabila, was born in August 1998 as soon as the war started. This group is especially interesting because it was illustrative of the mutations of actors and aims. The RCD was initially led by Ernest Wamba-dia-Wamba and strongly backed by Rwanda and Uganda. Less than a year later, the RCD progressively split due to a lack of cohesion and the opportunistic logics of its leaders, and also due to the tensions between Rwanda and Uganda. The first split happened in May 1999, when Wamba-dia-Wamba created the RCD-Kisangani (RCD-K, or RCD-Wamba, or RCD-ML). But very quickly, Wamba-dia-Wamba was removed from his function and replaced by Mbusa Nyamwisi. This first split actually reflected the tension between Uganda and Rwanda, which were fighting over the control of Kisangani and its diamond-oriented economy.

The second split happened with the creation of a second faction, the RCD-Goma (RCD-G), led by Emile Ilunga. This division seemed to be, among other things, "the result of Uganda's divide-and-rule tactics."[163] At the end, RCD-Goma, backed by Rwanda, was controlling southern North Kivu, South Kivu, Maniema, Kisangani, North Katanga, Kasaï Occidental, and Kisangani. RCD-ML, backed by Uganda, was controlling Ituri and northern North Kivu. Behind these mutations, one must also see Ugandan and Rwandan changes of perspective; besides, the "Six Day War" of Kisangani is a symbol of the evolution in Uganda-Rwanda positions. Far from being fixed and coherent, the trajectory of the RCD and its factions reflects how multiple and changing the purpose of their fighting was.

Oscillating between political, ethnic, economic, power, and survival interests, the warring parties, alliances, and leaders changed throughout the conflict. There was no limited number of actors with fixed aims and defined positions. It was rather a fluctuant mix of actors and aims. As presented, each actor had its

---

[163] Koen Vlassenroot and Timothy Raeymaekers, eds., *Conflict and Social Transformation in Eastern DR Congo* (Ghent: Academia Press, 2004), 51.

own complex trajectory that changed its positioning in the conflict. Accordingly, the conflict changed with the actors' mutations. Even if it is true that some actors kept a certain regularity in their aims, there is not a unique and clear approach to understanding the entire conflict because of this global complexity, these mutations, and this generativeness. To conclude, the variations of warring parties had a determinant impact on the war itself by modifying the purposes of the war.

War System

The complexity of the Second Congo War and its various purposes must be understood in the light of the new dynamics which appeared during the conflict. The war created new political, economic, structural, and cultural logics. For instance, war opened the door to new ways of earning money. War also destroyed many cultural, economic, and political patterns, and it obliged the population to create new ones in order to survive the war. Illegal exploitation and smuggling were not only planned by some warlords and militias, but these were also ways for people to survive. Political goals became harder to distinguish and to isolate. The trajectories of the various groups and their leaders were very confused. War became a system, producing new elements, new strategies, new perspectives, new goals, and thus changing the war itself.

Economy Throughout War

The Second Congo War is sadly known for its economic aspect. As Jacques Lamarche said, "Profits are good as long as war lasts! War lasts as long as entrepreneurs find it profitable."[164] The economy gradually became one of the main

---

[164] Translation from the original quote: "Les profits sont intéressants tant que dure la guerre! La guerre dure tant que des entrepreneurs y trouvent leurs

pillars of the conflict. For many actors – states, leaders, warlords, militias, and ordinary people – this war was transformed into a way to earn money and to access natural resources – mainly cobalt, coltan, copper, diamonds, and gold. A new economic system in terms of structure, actors, and dynamics was born throughout the war.

As explained in *RDC: Rêve ou Illusion?*, behind the African solidarity and supposed security reasons lay political and economic interests. Each country, like every group, had its own interests, its own networks, and its own way of using natural resources in the conflict. Reports issued by a United Nations group of experts in 2000 at the request of the President of the UN Security Council exposed the different channels for financing and exploiting that each group used.

The "Six Day War" episode reflected the complexity and interests of this conflict. The two foreign armies from Rwanda and Uganda, theoretically on the same side, fought each other on Congolese soil in Kisangani from June 5 to 10, 2000. Clearly, this geographically strategic city was a very important place for trade, gold, and diamond mining, which was the source of the conflict. Natural resources were a key factor.

In this African-style Far West, every country involved in the war tried to set up networks to maintain their influence, even after they had withdrawn their troops, to continue exploiting natural resources.

Elsewhere, four out of the ten African countries engaged in the war were involved at a very high level in illegal trafficking of natural resources in the conflict, namely the DRC, Uganda, Rwanda, and Zimbabwe. Many companies were also involved. Some 85 firms from all over the world (Belgium, Canada, China, Finland, France, Germany, Israel, Kazakhstan, Malaysia, Netherlands, South Africa, Switzerland, United Arab Emirates, and the United States), many of them multinationals,

---

profits." Jacques Lamarche, *La dynastie des Lanthiers* (Montréal: Pierre Tisseyre, 1973).

were mentioned in the report by the UN panel of experts[165] because they violated international law in the conflict.

At a smaller and more local level, the economy also invaded the conflict. As Roberto Beneduce, Luca Jourdan, Timothy Raeymaekers, and Koen Vlassenroot point out:

> (T)he seeming intractability of the Congolese conflict can only be fully understood with reference to:
>
> 1. the ways in which conflict has reshaped structures of opportunity and meaning at the level of 'grassroots' interaction and;
>
> 2. ...the motivations of the perpetrators of violence at the individual level.
>
> ...(V)iolence can be understood both as local discourse and a means to get access to public and private goods, which in turn has reshaped local rural societies.[166]

The war economy must therefore be understood as a means of subsistence and not only as a leader's or rebel's way to make a profit. Populations adapted to and accommodated the war. Life does not stop with war, people find ways to survive. Vlassenroot and Raeymaeckers rightly argue that the general state of disorder offered the necessary conditions for the formation of new patterns of local economic control and rearticulated the linkages between economic networks and identity.[167] Consequently, populations indirectly may have started to play a role in the development or the maintaining of the conflict, for instance by paying rebel groups in exchange for protection. Populations or neutral groups may thus have contributed to fueling the tensions by feeding some groups and by developing parallel systems. This modified the balance of power and the stakes at work in the conflict.

---

[165] United Nations, *Final Report of the Panel of Experts on the Illegal Exploitation of Natural Resources and Other Forms of Wealth of the Democratic Republic of the Congo* (S/2002/1146, October 2002).
[166] Beneduce, Jourdan, Raeymaekers, and Vlassenroot, "Violence with a purpose," 33.
[167] *cf.* Vlassenroot and Raeymaekers, *Conflict and Social Transformation.*

In the end, economics corrupted the conflict. It modified the actors' logics and social, political, and cultural systems. As a result, the conflict changed.

War Complex

Economics is not an independent sphere; it is fully embedded in the social and political life of society. The evolution of economic logics and systems, as has been explained above, go hand in hand with political and cultural changes. Along these lines, Vlassenroot and Raeymaeckers develop and apply to the DRC the notion of a "war complex" to explain the birth of new structures of power, profit, and protection in war.

Vlassenroot and Raeymaeckers base their approach on the concept of "complexes of power" developed by Christopher Parker.[168] Parker uses this term in order to highlight the nonlinearity of political and socio-economic changes. Rather than being transformed in a uniform way by following processes of diffusion from "centers" to "peripheries," or from "above" to "below," political and socio-economic systems mutate with "gaps and lags" in time and space. The consequence is the production of "emergent effects of power, opportunity, and meaning."[169]

The two authors thus define these complexes of power, profit, and protection as:

> parallel governance structures that function next to the formal state apparatus to foster an independent process of politico-military control, of redistribution or economic resources and right to wealth.[170]

---

[168] *Ibid.*, 14.
[169] *Ibid.*, 14.
[170] *Ibid.*, 23.

The emergence of these new "complexes" explains the persistence, the complexity, and the fluidity of the conflict. The Congolese "war complex" is not a blackout in a situation of peace, it is rather the creation of new dynamics and new social realties with a durable impact. Following David Keen's opinion, it is necessary to move beyond the idea of war-as-breakdown toward a fresh look about how people, local elites, and international governments are constantly adapting to war.

In a similar vein, David J. Francis underlines the generativeness of these complex war situations.

> The positive role and activities of some of the security/defense and socio-developmental civil society forces and organizations in war-torn and transition societies demonstrate that, far from disintegrating, civil society in these complex political emergencies have shown a remarkable resilience in providing public goods for the community and even necessities for existence.[171]

The Congolese War was precisely this kind of complex event, giving rise to multiple and complex logics. The emergence of these new logics interacting with older ones underlines the dimensionality of this war.

The focus of this chapter was to understand and grasp the mutations of the reasons to fight throughout the Second Congo War. So, what conclusions can be drawn? Warring parties and their trajectories changed over the course of the war and gave birth to new socio-cultural, economic, and political dynamics and logics. The war was neither linear nor stable, but rather a CAS. Its purpose changed along the course of the conflict because new actors appeared, other disappeared, some changed, and each of them had its own reasons to fight; as a consequence, the war itself changed. In other words, this conflict was a fluid, multiple, evolving, generative, and

---

[171] David J. Francis, ed., *Civil Militia: Africa's Intractable Security Menace?* (Aldershot: Ashgate, 2005), 19.

nonlinear event, in which agents mutated and changed the war itself.

The initial reasons for the war were already numerous and intertwined. But as soon as the war started, leaders, countries, alliances, militias, and rebel groups shifted in their forms and their objectives. Economics progressively corrupted the conflict. But economics was fully embedded in other socio-political features – ethnic, cultural, political, ideological, local, regional, national, international – which alternated in space and time as elements of the conflict. Countries' positioning and strategies changed throughout the conflict, as was shown for Rwanda, Uganda, and the DRC. It has equally been explained that countries were fighting for very different reasons, from economics for Zimbabwe to domestic stability for Angola to recognition for Libya. Groups such as RCD knew numerous and substantial mutations in structure, and consequently in purpose. The various political, cultural, local, and ethnic groups, such as Maï-Maï and Interahamwe, used and/or were used in the conflict. Moreover, in the new context of the war, people could not behave and think in the same way. Indeed, survival and other priorities took the upper hand because the situation became gloomy, the future uncertain, and life riskier. Almost each warring party changed during the war. Similar to a ballet, new actors entered and exited, changing décor and costumes, and all this governed by the rhythms of different pieces of music.

CHAPTER 7
THE US-VIETNAM WAR (1954-1973)

The United States was in Vietnam because it was there.[172]
– Martin van Creveld

The Vietnam War lasted around twenty-five years. It started in the early 1950s and US involvement ended in 1973, two years before the fall of Saigon brought the war to a definitive close. All in all, it involved five US administrations – those of Harry S. Truman (1945-1953), Dwight D. Eisenhower (1953-1961), John F. Kennedy (1961-1963), Lyndon B. Johnson (1963-1969), and Richard Nixon (1969-1974). Fully embedded in the Cold War, the US went to war mainly to fight communism.

The Vietnam War, although it seems to be a much more stable conflict because of its place in the global and apparently fixed pattern of the Cold War, and because of its state-centric nature, was nonetheless a complex conflict which experienced mutations. The strategic and political purpose of the war evolved throughout its duration.

However, this example differs from the Congolese war, and this chapter approaches it differently. For the Second Congo War, we analyzed multiple warring parties and the overall dynamics. In contrast, this chapter will focus only on the American actor. Elsewhere, the Vietnam War was a more clearly delimited and uniform war in terms of actors and purpose. Indeed, the actors were less numerous, more coherent, and less changing. The Cold War pattern limited the global purpose of the Vietnam war because it was providing a guiding

---

[172] Creveld, *Transformation of War*, 147.

line. Most of the strategic and political choices made were embedded in and determined by the Cold War. The logical consequence is that this restricts the possibility of bringing out the mutations of war's purpose. Nevertheless, our analytical pattern remains valid. The complexity and mutations were less pronounced and more subtle, but still present. This research deliberately focuses on a state, which is by nature more stable and robust, and on a more "ossified" period. It will show that, even in this case, the Vietnam War was still an uncertain and self-modifying social phenomenon, *i.e.*, a CAS.

The Morass of Vietnam

To say that we are closer to victory today is to believe, in the face of the evidence, the optimists who have been wrong in the past. To suggest we are on the edge of defeat is to yield to unreasonable pessimism. To say that we are mired in the stalemate seems the only realistic, yet unsatisfactory, conclusion.[173]

– Walter Cronkite

In 1946, the French started to fight in Vietnam in what is often called the First Indochina War (or French Indochina War). It was mainly a colonial war. The French fought to hold on to their colony in Vietnam, whereas Viet Minh were fighting for independence and other interests. The war took shape while the Cold War spectrum progressively loomed on the horizon. Consequently, the US, although skeptical towards these kinds of colonial conflict, progressively took a keen interest in the matter. In this way, in 1949 and 1950, "the US shifted from neutrality to open and soon massive support for the French."[174]

---

[173] Walter Cronkite, "We Are Mired in Stalemate," February 27, 1968, in *Landmark Speeches on the Vietnam War*, ed. Gregory Allen Olson (College Station: Texas A&M University Press, 2010), 125.
[174] George C. Herring, *America's Longest War: The United States and Vietnam, 1950–1975*, 4th ed. (New York: McGraw-Hill, 2002), 15.

On the other side, the Soviet Union and communist China were helping the Viet Minh.

Backing France in Vietnam with military and economic assistance came to be considered as a key element for the security of Western Europe, among other things because Vietnam was viewed by many American strategists as the key to keeping Southeast Asia out of communist hands.[175] The domino theory[176] was becoming more and more prevalent. "By 1952, the United States was bearing roughly one-third of the cost of the war, but it was dissatisfied with the results and with its inability to influence French military policy."[177]

From then on, things took a different turn for various reasons: French reluctance to continue the war; bad results in the field; increasing importance of the domino theory and fear of communism; and the new Eisenhower administration. At the 1954 Geneva conference and following the fall of Dien Bien Phu, lost by the French, a temporary partition of Vietnam was decided. This is how the French Indochina War ended, whereas the US-Vietnam war had actually already started.

Vietnam was divided in two; the US remained involved and firmly determined to maintain control over the country and to prevent communism from expanding. In this way, they strongly backed Ngo Dinh Diem, president of South Vietnam from 1955 to 1963. However, insurrection in the South grew, and Diem was not successful in controlling it.

The arrival of the Kennedy administration did not improve the situation; in contrast, it led to the US becoming more bogged down in the war. "Inheriting from Eisenhower an increasingly dangerous if still limited commitment, he [Kennedy] plunged deeper into the morass,"[178] as George C.

---

[175] *Ibid.*, 20.
[176] The domino theory was a Cold War theory developed and promoted by the United States. This theory especially concerned Asia. It speculated that if one state in a region came under the influence of communism, then the surrounding countries would follow in a domino effect.
[177] Herring, *America's Longest War*, 27.
[178] *Ibid.*, 91.

Herring stated. During the Kennedy and Johnson administrations, the domino theory had been supplanted by the notion of credibility and posture.[179] Even if they were aware of the difficulty (and maybe the impossibility) of winning the war, they did not want to abandon the struggle. After the three-part crisis of 1961 – the failure of the Bay of Pigs invasion, the construction of the Berlin Wall, and a negotiated settlement between the pro-western government of Laos and the Pathet Lao communist movement – Kennedy believed that another failure on the part of the US would fatally damage US credibility with its allies as well as his own reputation. Thus, Kennedy decided to increase the amount of American assistance through the number of advisers, money, equipment, and training.

The situation in Vietnam worsened, notably during the first months of Johnson's presidency. Thus, between November 1963 and July 1965, Johnson progressively transformed the assistance to the South Vietnamese government into "an open-ended commitment to preserve an independent, non-Communist South Vietnam."[180] In 1965, the beginning of operation Rolling Thunder, Operation Starlight, and the deployment of many US combat units illustrated this major shift in the war. This is how the Vietnam War became an active and open battlefront.

From then on, the war escalated, involving more and more US soldiers. A peak of more than 540,000 US soldiers was reached at the end of 1968.[181] In the meantime, the US was moving forward in the war in a vague and uncertain way, tossed about by events. Also, it underestimated the enemy's capacity to resist and the difficulties raised by the terrain and the climate, and it was not really prepared for unconventional warfare.

In the US, public opinion and the media were becoming increasingly critical of the war. In 1968, even if the US

---

[179] George C. Herring, "America and Vietnam: The Unending War," *Foreign Affairs* 70, no.5 (Winter 1991), 108.
[180] Herring, *America's Longest War*, 131.
[181] Stanley Karnow, *Vietnam: A History*, 2nd ed. (New York: Penguin, 1997), 697.

successfully fought back the Tet Offensive – when the North Vietnamese army and the Viet Cong (a guerrilla force) launched coordinated attacks in the South in order to demonstrate that the North was far from defeated – Americans were shocked and the Johnson administration was strongly affected. In 1969, Johnson's successor, Richard Nixon, was in a difficult situation with the war and developed a new doctrine often called "Vietnamization." The strategy was to buy time, to start a progressive withdrawal, and to allow the South Vietnamese armed forces to build up their strength so they could defend themselves. So, troop withdrawals started and never stopped until the US was fully out of the war. In the end, Nixon's aim was to disengage without losing face while still limiting the spread of communism.

On January 27, 1973, the Paris Peace Accords on "ending the war and restoring peace in Vietnam" were signed and officially ended direct US involvement in the Vietnam War.

To conclude, the US had been progressively dragged into the Vietnam quagmire. The inertia of the conflict prevented any easy way out, or a simple withdrawal and a new start. The more the US moved forward in the war, the more each administration took decisions not only focusing on the initial strategic purpose of the war, but on the side effects of the war. It would be misleading to say that the main focus of this war, to stem communism, had been bypassed. However, the specific reasons for this war tended to be forgotten. Initially a "tactical part" of a global strategy against communism, the Vietnam War came to be a strategic event in itself. It is similar to starting a fire for whatever reason, but when the smoke it produces becomes the main concern, one forgets why the fire was started in the first place. Day after day, administration after administration, the way out of the Vietnam War became more and more difficult. The war slowly but surely gained weight in US domestic and foreign policies and thus became an increasing political tool and threat at the same time.

From its beginnings, the fact that the war got progressively bogged down points out the autonomous logic that developed throughout the conflict. Rather than responding to a clear and independent state reason, the conflict became a system with a new and autonomous logic of its own.

A Domestic Fight

The Vietnam War came to be a US domestic issue, which subsequently contributed to change the face of the war itself. "Few wars in American history have had as profound and lasting influence on domestic politics, culture, and economics as the Vietnam War"[182] wrote Melvin Small. More than a post-battle effect, home became a "front-line" during the war. The prolonged length of the Vietnam War made it progressively weigh more and more in domestic policy. Ergo, it became a stake, a threat, and a tool in domestic political struggles.

As Herring wrote, "no administration…could survive the loss of Vietnam."[183] Besides the international strategic aims of the war, domestic policy had become a central matter in the conflict. Obviously, this was a two-way road; in other words, the war affected national politics as well as the opposite. So, the purpose of the Vietnam War changed and was muddled by the weight of domestic interests.

In all the US elections and campaigns from the 1950s to the 1970s, the Vietnam War marked debates and political struggles. It was clearly a strategic issue.

During the campaign of 1952, the Republicans had attacked the Truman administration for failing to stop the advance of communism, and declared that "they [the Republicans] were even more determined than their predecessors to prevent the fall of Indochina."[184] However, the change claimed by the Eisenhower administration was more a change "of mood

---

[182] Melvin Small, *At the Water's Edge: American Politics and the Vietnam War* (Lanham: Ivan R Dee, 2006), 3.
[183] Herring, "America and Vietnam," 109.
[184] *Ibid.*, 30.

and tactics rather than substance,"[185] at least at the beginning of his presidency.

As Eisenhower did eight years before, Kennedy campaigned by accusing the administration of not being efficient enough against the communist threat. Very concerned by the Vietnam issue since his first visit to that country in 1951, Kennedy labeled in 1956 America's stake in Vietnam as "the cornerstone of the free world in Southeast Asia."[186] However, according to Herring, Kennedy was hesitant and provisional rather than decisive and carefully calculated concerning Vietnam policy issues.[187] In 1963, the Buddhist crisis (a period of repression of Buddhists by the South Vietnamese government) strongly divided the Kennedy administration.

Right after Kennedy's assassination in November 1963, the new president, Johnson, feared that rapid and large-scale involvement could threaten his chances of election in 1964. Presidents Truman, Eisenhower, and Kennedy had not officially intervened in hostilities in Southeast Asia, even if they had laid the groundwork for such action. In contrast, just a few months after his election, Johnson decided to follow the advice of the National Security Council to deploy combat troops. Frederik Logevall explains that it is essential to understand the duality in Johnson's thinking about the war, in which partisan calculations competed for supremacy with concerns for his personal reputation, in order to grasp his fifteen first months.[188] By and large, Johnson tended to personalize all issues relating to the war and this tendency "was there from the start, from the time he vowed to not be the first American president to lose a

---

[185] *Ibid.*, 30.
[186] John F. Kennedy, "America's Stake in Vietnam: The Cornerstone of the Free World in Southeast Asia," June 1, 1956, in *Landmark Speeches on the Vietnam War*, ed. Gregory Allen Olson (College Station: Texas A&M University Press, 2010), 19.
[187] Herring, "America and Vietnam," 90-91.
[188] Fredrik Logevall, *Choosing War: The Lost Chance for Peace and the Escalation of War in Vietnam* (Berkeley: University of California Press, 2001), 391.

war."[189] Longevall continues by saying that "it would be difficult to exaggerate the importance of this conflation of the national interest and his own personal interest in Johnson's approach to Vietnam."[190] By late 1967, around 500,000 Americans were fighting in Vietnam, and thousands of them were dying every month. Thus, a major factor in the decline of Johnson's popularity was the Vietnam War.

Once again in 1968, the Vietnam War played a role in US elections, but in this case it was even more crucial. "Few elections in American history were so dominated by foreign policy, and few elections so strongly influenced foreign policy during a campaign,"[191] Small explains. Declarations, plans, and decisions about the war needed to take into account the domestic situation. At that time, public opinion was divided, and the domestic situation was tense – racial issues, riots, anti-war movements, strong activism, Martin Luther King's assassination. Representing a calmer society, Nixon promised peace with honor: "I pledge to you that new leadership will end the war and win the peace in the Pacific."[192] So, Nixon was elected and took office on January 20, 1969. In this context, Nixon progressively ended the war while trying not to lose it – at least, on the face of it.

Another aspect of the home front, however, correlated to the election aspect described above: public opinion (although this designation must be used cautiously because the term is vague and the notion elusive). On November 15, 1969, the US experienced the largest anti-war rally in its history; 300,000 protesters mobilized through this mass demonstration in Washington, DC. There had been an uprising among a substantial number of Americans who interacted and played a key role by influencing the decision-making process of the Vietnam War. Public opinion was thus a part of what can be called a *home front complex*.

---

[189] *Ibid.*, 392.
[190] *Ibid.*, 392.
[191] Small, *At The Water's Edge*, 124.
[192] Richard Nixon, in Rick Perlstein, "Not in his father's footsteps," *Los Angeles Times* (February 10, 2008).

The relationship between the Vietnam War and domestic politics shows that the war was a social phenomenon, which was multiple, unpredictable, and self-modifying, and which mobilized, changed, and produced change. The Vietnam War acquired a domestic policy dimension, which in turn changed the war itself.

Reasons for War: From the Origins to the End

"One of the best examples of what happens when linearity meets nonlinearity in this century took place in Vietnam,"[193] Thomas J. Czerwinski argues. Behind the logic of the global war on communism led by the US, the Vietnam War experienced many mutations. Far from being one unit with a regular pattern and some changes in terms of tactics, this war was an adventure (whatever may be the personal opinions on its necessity and success). Through two angles – the progressive entry into the quagmire, and the opening of a domestic front – it was shown how the conflict experienced mutations of its purpose. The reasons for fighting the war changed.

In the early fifties, at the commencement of the conflict, the key purpose was clearly the struggle against communism. However, even in this perspective, the centrality of Vietnam was not so obvious at the beginning. Amid many other countries in Southeast Asia, Vietnam became the most important in the region for the United States. This shift happened progressively from the end of the forties until the mid-fifties. "The first commitment in Vietnam, a commitment to help the French suppress the Vietminh revolution, was part of this broader attempt to contain communist expansion in Asia."[194] After the French departure, the US continued and increased its involvement. Thus, Vietnam came to be considered as strategic, and the domino theory was there to

---

[193] Czerwinski, *Coping with the Bounds*, 32.
[194] Herring, "America and Vietnam," 107.

underline the importance of the country in the fight against communism.

In the Kennedy and Johnson administrations, the background was still the communist threat, but the war became much more a matter of credibility, posture, and image. It was capital to appear firm and strong, certainly not weak. They gradually increased the scale of the American effort, and avoided answering "the toughest question – whether to accept the true costs of victory or defeat."[195]

The domestic issue began to weigh more. As Herring wrote, "the fall of Vietnam to communism would have disastrous political consequences at home"[196] – in other words, it was essential for any administration not to lose in Vietnam. Since 1965, when Johnson openly sent US combat forces to Vietnam for the first time, the importance of the domestic aspects in the purpose of the war continuously increased until the US ended its involvement in 1973.

To conclude, the Vietnam War did not unfold as planned. Day after day, year after year, administration after administration, the war developed progressively through its own inertia. It is indeed difficult to tell whether the presidents and their administrations were leading the war, or following its caprices. Starting around the 1950s, the war took many unforeseen directions. It started as a limited intervention to keep Southeast Asia out of the communist hands that very few Americans were aware of. It then became a major symbolic struggle against communism, and a substantial domestic issue. It mutated according to many variables, from domestic issues to foreign policy to the president's personal decisions. Ultimately, the effects of the war, domestic and international, impacted the logic of the war itself.

Politics and war were engaged in a dialectical and dynamic relationship. The war began for specific political

---

[195] Gideon Rose, *How Wars End – Why We Always Fight the Last Battle* (New York: Simon & Schuster, 2010), 9.
[196] Herring, "America and Vietnam," 108.

reasons, but as soon as it started, it changed politics, which in turn changed the war. Thus, the Vietnam War was a CAS, despite the fact that it was less changing and complex than the Second Congo War.

CONCLUSION

War is understood in the framework of the one analyzing it. In this sense, contemporary political and strategic thinkers consider the war phenomenon through their biased lenses. Modern democratic states and their views are challenged by contemporary conflicts. The main purpose of this book is to widen their perspectives, to unlock their confinement, to give them new windows of reflection. Because behind these biased perspectives are hidden democratic contradictions and strategic misconducts.

Reviewing some of the most influential theories on war since Machiavelli – Hobbes, Kant, Montesquieu, Clausewitz, Marxist-Leninist theories, Waltz, Wendt, economic perspectives, and peace research – this work underlines their lack of focus on the multi-dimensionality of war. By understanding their limits, it analyzes how they tend to fix war in order to make it manageable. They all judge war, and want to give it a specific meaning or direction, and/or they want to define its causes, reasons, or effects. In other words, most of them are teleological, meaning they are goal-oriented in one way or another. So, in the end, they simplify war in terms of time, space, interaction, purpose, aim, and evolution. In contrast to these theories, this book conceptualizes war as a CAS. By discussing the social, temporal, and spatial dimensions of war, it exposes its complexity, unpredictability, changes, and autonomy. Accordingly, my research shows how, in war, the agents and the system are adaptive because the individual and collective behaviors of its agents change as a result of experience, which has repercussions on war itself. War comes to resemble an "ecosystem," where living organisms are continually engaged in a set of relationships with every other element constituting their environment. Thus, war can be understood as a generative social phenomenon, which is accordingly uncertain and self-modifying – or, said differently, a CAS.

The analysis of two very different wars – the Second Congo War and the Vietnam War until the end of US involvement – demonstrates the pertinence of a CAS-based approach. As soon as the Second Congo War started, leaders, countries, alliances, militias, and rebel groups shifted in their forms and their objectives. Economics progressively corrupted the conflict, while being embedded in other socio-political features – ethnic, cultural, political, ideological, local, regional, national, international – which changed in space and time. Starting in the 1950s, the Vietnam War took many unforeseen directions before it ended more than twenty years later. It started as a limited intervention to keep Southeast Asia out of communist hands, then became a major symbolic struggle against communism, then a substantial domestic controversy in the US. It mutated according to many variables, spanning domestic issues to foreign policy to the personal decisions of presidents. In each of these two examples, politics and war were engaged in a dialectical and dynamic relationship. Agents mutated, which in turn changed the war. These wars show how and why war can be considered as a CAS.

This book expounds the shortcomings in the common understanding of war following a transversal approach, specifically by gathering knowledge of political philosophy, international relations, military studies, and sociology. Each field examines war through its own lens, ignoring many facets of the phenomenon. The two main academic areas interested in war are currently international relations and military studies. International relations are teleological because they tend to establish patterns and paradigms. They focus on the whole system and its linearity; variations, change, and uncertainty globally take a back seat. Phenomena are not analyzed so much for what they are, but much more for how they can contribute to a global understanding of the international system. In a different manner, military studies have a relatively similar bias. They are practically oriented and consequently equally teleological. The conduct of war is their main focus. They are limited in their comprehension of the war phenomenon. This study has aimed to offset these trends. To do so, based on a political philosophy pattern, both international relations and military studies were used, following a sociological perspective.

"And so what?" Indeed, one could argue that this book ultimately brings the reader back to the starting point. Apart from underlining the vast disorder prevailing in war, what does it bring? Indeed, since this research focuses on complexity, change, and uncertainty, one could think that it is antithetical to action, that it promotes the status quo, and that it merely underlines a vacuum of knowledge concerning war and its mechanisms. These views are mistaken. As General Martin E. Dempsey said, "the most successful soldiers have not been those who avoided war's uncertainty, but rather those who embraced it so that it worked in their favor."[197] Also, it must not give rise to the praise of short-term thinking. As Christopher Coker[198] interestingly pointed out, in our liquid societies people live in an age of risk; they are constantly preoccupied by the fear of uncertainty and the complexity of the contemporary world. Consequently, they live in the short term and fear the danger inherent to life itself.

The analysis of war presented in this research is far from promoting inaction, fear, or short-term actions, which could all be considered from the complexity and nonlinearity of war. In contrast, what it can do is contribute to an evolution of decision-making processes at the political, strategic, and military levels thanks to a better understanding of war, its making, and its consequences. It aims to open the door to a more dynamic approach to war, which is essential in contemporary times because threats take new forms and confuse our points of reference,[199] and also because contemporary western democracies make people think that there is a clear and unique *reason of state* guiding war. In

---

[197] Gen. Martin E. Dempsey, Foreword, in *Between War and Peace: How America Ends its Wars*, ed. Matthhew Moten (New York: Free Press, 2011), vii.
[198] Christopher Coker, *War in an Age of Risk* (Cambridge: Polity Press, 2009).
[199] Such as the distinctions between tactical, operational, strategic, and political levels, which tend to become blurred.

practice, the reason of state is composite, changing, and affected by the circumstances of war and its various interests. Each day of war changes war. Ends and means constantly interrelate, causes and consequences are intertwined, because in reality war is not one event but a set of micro-events. This perspective can assist us in better understanding the complexity of contemporary conflicts as well as their various patterns and mutations. Wars are ongoing processes in constant evolution. War is alive.

Pursuing this line of reasoning further, this book exposes the contemporary strategic vacuum, as well as encourages decision makers to improve their long-term policies on war and their political and strategic thinking. It confronts theory to realities, strategic ideals to war's complexity. The denouement of war is at play in the details of its making, where its designers never set foot. This breach between theory and practice draws attention to the schizophrenia and the contradictions of contemporary western democratic states. They believe they are farsighted, but they are flawed in short-term policy and stuck in the morass of their own wars. They claim to promote great ideals, however they neither fully respect them nor do they reach out to peacefully share them. They hide the facts (torture, clandestine operations, political failures) that do not fit into their ideals. Through new technology, they measure and rationalize in order to control, forecast and be protected. But they do not have a better grasp on war mechanisms, and are confronted with their own strategic flaws and lack of political coherence. Finally, they are trapped in their own political and strategic logics during war. This is amplified by structures arising from electoral logics, ideological rigidity, bureaucratic heaviness, institutional deadlocks, internal clientelism, slow decision-making processes, deep inertia – which all narrow their views and mobility, intellectually and practically, in war.

Furthermore, the culture of emotions and instantaneous public opinion complicates any long-term thinking. As a consequence, the apparent political coherence of these states breaks up during war. The dilemma remains in finding the balance between the need for long-term views and the constant fluidity of contemporary conflicts and security issues – and this dilemma seems inextricable. It would require an ideological shift from democratic states. By keeping away from the reality of war – its complexity, its multiple facets, its mechanisms, its contradictions, its reasons, its necessity, its violence – fantasies and ideals about war persist and corrupt the pertinence of our decisions. Simplification is at work. It is as if states were living in a strategic utopia, blinding themselves and remaining stuck on solely tactical details.

In contrast, democracies should understand that war is a CAS, it is change by essence. Then, they should agree on it among themselves in order to allow states to act accordingly. They have to improve their long-term thinking in uncertain and fluid contexts, rather than being paralyzed by them. CAS is a tool that must alert them to the change that inevitably happens in war, and that must lead modern democracies to develop sharper long-term views to confront the inconsistencies of war. That said, the question remains: in the current global system, are our modern democratic states really able to be transparent, reactive, and ideologically, politically, and operationally adaptive enough to make this ideological shift, and in doing so preserve democratic values and principles?

BIBLIOGRAPHY

Acker, Céline. "La 'scène' de la guerre ou la monstration des mécanismes chez Eschyle et Kant." *Sens Public* (February 2002). http://www/sens-public.org/spip.php?article132

Aeschylus. "The Persians." In *The Plays of Aeschylus*. 472 BC. Translated by Robert Potter, 4th ed. London: George Routledge and Sons, 1895.

Ainley, Kirsten, and Chris Brown. *Understanding International Relations*. 4th ed. Basingstoke: Palgrave Macmillan, 2009.

Alberts, David S., and Thomas J. Czerwinski, eds. *Complexity, Global Politics, and National Security*. Washington, DC: National Defense University, 1997.

Arendt, Hannah. *Crises of the Republic: Lying in Politics, Civil Disobedience; On Violence; Thoughts on Politics and Revolution*. New York: Harcourt Brace Jovanovich, 1972.

------. *On Violence*. New York: Harcourt Publishers, 1970.

------. *The Human Condition*. 1958. Reprint, London: University of Chicago Press, 1998.

------. *The Promise of Politics*. New York: Schocken, 2005.

Aron, Raymond. *La guerre en chaîne*. 3rd ed. Paris: Gallimard, 1951.

------. *Penser la guerre, Clausewitz – 1. L'âge européen*. Paris: Gallimard, 1976.

------. *Penser la guerre, Clausewitz – 2. L'âge planétaire*. Paris: Gallimard, 1976.

Atlan, Henri. "L'intuition du complexe et ses théorisations." In *Les théories de la complexité, Autour de l'œuvre d'Henri Atlan*. Paris: Seuil, 1991.

------. *Le vivant post-génomique ou Qu'est-ce que l'auto-organisation?* Paris: Odile Jacob, 2011.

Axelrod, Robert. "Building New Political Actors: A Model for the Emergence of New Political Actors." In *Artificial Societies: the Computer Simulation of Social Life*, edited by Nigel Gilbert and Rosaria Conte. London: University College Press, 1995.

------. *The Evolution of Cooperation*. 2nd ed. Cambridge, MA: Basic Books, 2006.

Bandura, Albert. *Self-efficacy: The Exercise of Control*. New York: W.H. Freeman, 1997.

------. "Self-efficacy." In *Encyclopedia of Human Behavior*, edited by V. S. Ramachaudran. Vol.4:71-81. New York: Academic Press, 1994.
http://des.emory.edu/mfp/BanEncy.html

Battistella, Dario. *Théories des relations internationales*. 2nd ed. Paris: Presses de la Fondation nationale des sciences politiques, 2006.

Bauman, Zygmunt. "Wars of the Globalization Era." *European Journal of Social Theory* 4, no.1 (2001):11-28.

Baumard, Philippe. *Le vide stratégique*. Paris: CNRS Editions, 2012.

Council on Foreign Relations. "HBO History Makers Series with Stanley A. McChrystal." Video of a CFR meeting which took place on October 6, 2011.
http://www.cfr.org/defense-strategy/hbo-history-makers-series-stanley-mcchrystal-video/p26065

Beck, Ulrich. *Risk Society: towards a New Modernity*. London: Sage Publications, 1992.

Berdal, Mats. "How 'New' Are 'New Wars'? Global Economic Change and the Study of Civil War." *Global Governance* 9 (2003):477-502.

Bersini, Hugues. *Qu'est-ce que l'émergence?* Paris: Ellipses, 2007.

Beyerchen, Alan. "Clausewitz, Nonlinearity and the Unpredictability of War." *International Security* 17, no.3 (Winter 1992):59-90.

Bodin, Jean. *Six Books of the Commonwealth*. 1576. Translated by M.J. Tooley. Reprint, New York: Macmillan, 1955.

Bouthoul, Gaston. *Le phénomène guerre*. 1962. Reprint, Paris: Payot, 2006.

Buckley-Zistel, Susanne. "In-Between War and Peace: Identities, Boundaries and Change after Violent Conflict." *Millennium: Journal of International Studies* 35, no.1 (2006):3-24.

Burpo, F. John. "The Great Captains of Chaos: Developing Adaptive Leaders." *Military Review* (January/February 2006):64-70.

Callois, Roger. *Bellone ou La pente de la guerre*. Saint Clément de Rivière: Fata Morgana, 1994.

------. *L'homme et le sacré*. Paris: Flammarion, 1988.

Caplow, Theodore, and Louis Hicks. *Systems of War and Peace*. Lanham: University Press of America, 2002.

Cashman, Greg. *What Causes War? An Introduction to Theories of International Conflict*. New York: Lexington Books, 1993.

Clausewitz, Carl von. *On War: The Complete Edition*. Translated by Colonel J.J. Graham. Rockville: Wildside Press, 2009.

Codevilla, Angelo and Paul Seubury. *War: End and Means*. 2nd ed. Dulles: Potomac Books, 2006.

Coker, Christopher. *War in an Age of Risk*. Cambridge: Polity Press, 2009.

Collier, Paul. *The Bottom Billion: Why the Poorest Countries are Failing and What Can Be Done About It.* New York: Oxford University Press, 2008.

------, and Dominic Rohner. "Democracy, Development, and Conflict." *Journal of the European Economic Association* 6, no.2-3 (2008):531-540.

------, Anke Hoeffler and Dominic Rohner. *Beyond Greed and Grievance: Feasibility and Civil War*. Working paper, CSAE - University of Oxford (2006).

Colonomos, Ariel. *La Pari de la guerre: Guerre préventive, guerre juste?* Paris: Denoël, 2009.

------. *The Future as the Future of International Relations.* Conference given at the American University of Paris, Working Paper Series no.94, Paris, France, January 26, 2011.

Conteh-Morgan, Earl. *Collective Political Violence: An Introduction to the Theories and Cases of Violent Conflicts*. New York: Routledge, 2004.

Corning, Peter A. "The Re-Emergence of 'Emergence': A Venerable Concept in Search of a Theory." *Complexity* 7, no.6 (2002):18-30.

Creveld, Martin van. *The Transformation of War*. New York: Free Press, 1991.

Crocker, Chester A., Fen Osler Hampson, and Pamela Aall, eds. *Leashing the Dogs of War: Conflict Management in a Divided World*. Washington, DC: United States Institute of Peace, 2008.

Czerwinski, Thomas J. *Coping with the Bounds: A Neo-Clausewitzean Primer*. Revised ed. Washington, DC: DoD Command and Control Research Program, 2008.

Daintith, John, ed. *A Dictionary of Physics*. Oxford Reference Online. New York: Oxford University Press, 2009. Accessed June 21, 2011. https://acces-distant.sciences-po.fr:443/http/www.oxfordreference.com/views/ENTRY.html?subview=Main&entry=t83.e539

Damasio, Antonio R. *Descarte's Error: Emotion, Reason, and the Human Brain*. New York: Putnam Books, 1994.

Davis, Diane E., and Anthony W. Pereira, eds. *Irregular Armed Forces and Their Role in Politics and State Formation*. Cambridge: Cambridge University Press, 2004.

Dawson, Doyne. "The Origins of War: Biological and Anthropological Theories." *History and Theory* 35, no.1 (1996):1-28.

Desportes, Vincent. *Comprendre la guerre*. 2nd ed. Paris: Economica, 2001.

------. *Décider dans l'incertitude*. 2nd ed. Paris: Economica, 2007.

------. *La Guerre Probable: Penser autrement*. 2nd ed. Paris: Economica, 2008.

Deudney, Daniel H. *Bounding Power: Republican Security Theory from the Polis to the Global Village*. Princeton: Princeton University Press, 2007.

Deutsch, Morton. *The Resolution of Conflict: Constructive and Destructive Processes*. New Haven: Yale University Press, 1973.

Dillon, Michael, and Andrew W. Neal., eds. *Foucault on Politics, Security, and War*. New York: Palgrave Macmillan, 2008.

Dillon, Michael, and Julian Reid. *The Liberal Way of War: Killing to make life live*. London: Routledge, 2009.

Donnelly, Jack. *Realism and International Relations Theory*. Cambridge: Cambridge University Press, 2000.

Draper, Hal, and E. Haberkern. *Karl Marx's Theory of Revolution: Volume 5 – War and Revolution.* New York: Monthly Review Press, 2005.

Duffield, Mark. *Global Governance and the New Wars: The Merging of Development and Security.* London: Zed Books, 2006.

Dupuy, Kendra E., and Krijn Peters. *War and Children.* Santa Barbara: Praeger Security International, 2010.

Duyvesteyn, Isabelle, and Jan Angstrom, eds. *Rethinking the Nature of War.* London: Frank Cass, 2005.

Echevarriah, Antulio J. *Clausewitz and Contemporary War.* New York: Oxford University Press, 2009.

Ehrenreich, Barbara. *Le Sacre de la Guerre: Essai sur les passions du sang.* Paris: Calmann-Levy, 1999.

EspacesTemps Les Cahiers. *De la guerre: Un objet pour les sciences sociales*, no.71-72-73 (1999).

Farrell, Theo. "Constructivist Security Studies: Portrait of a Research Program." *International Studies Review* 4, no.1 (2002):49-72.

Fearon, James D., and David D. Laitin. "Violence and the Social Construction of Ethnic Identity. "*International Organization* 54, no.4 (Autumn 2000):845-877.

Fiala, Andrew. *Public War, Private Conscience: The Ethics of Political Violence.* London: Continuum, 2010.

Foucault, Michel. *Il faut défendre la société.* 1976. Reprint, Paris: Editions du Seuil, 1997.

------. *Society Must Be Defended.* 1976. Translated by David Macey. Reprint, New York: Picador, 2003.

Francart, Loup. "L'évolution des niveaux stratégique, opératif et tactique." *Stratégique* 68, no.4 (1997).

Francis, David J., ed. *Civil Militia: Africa's Intractable Security Menace?* Aldershot: Ashgate, 2005.

Freund, Julien. "Guerre et politique. De Karl von Clausewitz à Raymond Aron." *Revue française de sociologie* 17, no.4 (1976):643-651.

------. *L'essence du politique*. 3rd ed. Paris: Dalloz, 2003.

------. *Max Weber*. Paris: Presses Universitaires de France, 1969.

------. *Sociologie du conflit*. Paris: Presses Universitaires de France, 1983.

------. *Warfare in the Modern World: A Short But Critical Analysis*. Translated by Simona Draguhici. Washington, DC: Plutarch Press, 1996.

Gadamer, Hans-Georg. "Towards a Phenomenology of Ritual and Language." In *Language and Linguisticality in Gadamer's Hermeneutics*. Translated by Lawrence K. Schmidt and Monika Reuss. Lanham: Lexington Books, 2000.

------. *Langage et Vérité*. Translated by Jean-Claude Gens. Paris: Gallimard, 1995.

Gallie, Walter B. *Philosophers of Peace and War: Kant, Clausewitz, Marx, Engels and Tolstoy*. Cambridge: Cambridge University Press, 1978.

Galula, David. *Counterinsurgency Warfare: Theory and Practice*. 1964. Reprint, Westport: Praeger, 2006.

Gautier, Louis. *Face à la guerre*. Paris: La Table Ronde, 2006.

------. *La défense de la France après la guerre froide*. Paris: Presses Universitaires de France, 2009.

Gelven, Michael. *War and Existence*. University Park, PA: Pennsylvania University State Press, 1994.

Girard, René. *Achever Clausewitz*. Paris: Carnets Nord, 2007.

------. *Violence and the Sacred*. Translated by Patrick Gregory. Baltimore: Johns Hopkins University Press, 1977.

Giustozzi, Antonio. "Genesis of a 'Prince': The Rise of Ismail Khan in Western Afghanistan, 1979-1992." *Crisis State Working Papers,* DESTIN, LSE. No.4 (2006).

------. *Empires of Mud: Wars and Warlords in Afghanistan.* New York: Columbia University Press, 2009.

Goldstein, Jeffrey. "Emergence as a Construct: History and Issues." *Emergence: A Journal of Complexity Issues in Organizations and Management* 1, no.1 (1999):49-72.

Goya, Michel. *Sous le feu : Réflexion sur le comportement au combat.* Paris : CDEF-DREX, 2006

Gros, Frédéric. *Etats de violence: essai sur la fin de la guerre.* Paris: Gallimard, 2006.

Gupta, Dipak K. *Understanding Terrorism and Political Violence: The life cycle of birth, growth, transformation, and demise.* London: Routledge, 2008.

Haldi, Stacy Bergstrom. *Why Wars Widen: A Theory of Predation and Balancing.* London: Frank Cass, 2003.

Hassner, Pierre. "Les concepts de guerre et paix chez Kant." *Revue française de science politique* 11, no.3 (1961):642-670.

------, and Roland Marchal, eds. *Guerre et sociétés: Etat et violence après la Guerre Froide.* Paris: Karthala, 2003.

Heng, Yee-Kuang. *War as Risk Management: Strategy and Conflict in an Age of Globalised Risks.* London: Routledge, 2006.

Heraclitus. *Fragments.* In *The Art and Thought of Heraclitus: An Edition of the Fragments with Translation and Commentary.* Charles H. Kahn. Cambridge: Cambridge University Press, 1979.

Herberg-Rother, Andreas. *The re-politicization of war and violent conflicts.* Working paper, Fulda University of Applied Sciences. Accessed June 21, 2011. http://stockholm.sgir.eu

------, and Jan Willem Honig. "War without End(s): The End of Clausewitz?" *Distinktion: Scandinavian Journal of Social Theory* 15 (2007):133-150.

Herr, Michael. *Dispatches*. London: Pan Books, 1978.

Hobbes, Thomas. *Leviathan*. 1651. Reprint, London: Penguin Classics, 1985.

Holland, John Henry. *Hidden Order How Adaptation Builds Complexity*. Cambridge, MA: Perseus, 1996.

Howse, Robert. "Montesquieu on Commerce, Conquest, War, and Peace." *Brooklyn Journal of International Law* 31, no.3 (2006):693-708.

Hubin, Guy. *La Guerre, une vision française*. Paris: Economica, 2012.

Huddie, Leonie. "From Social to Political Identity: A Critical Examination of Social Identity Theory." *Political Psychology* 22, no.1 (2001):127-156.

Hutchings, Kimberly. *Time and World Politics*. Manchester: Manchester University Press, 2008.

Jabri, Vivienne. War and the Transformation of Global Politics. 2nd ed. New York: Palgrave Macmillan, 2010.

Jeong, Ho-Won. *Conflict Management and Resolution: An Introduction*. Oxon: Routledge, 2010.

Johnson, Neil. *Simply Complexity: A Clear Guide to Complexity Theory*. Oxford: Oneworld, 2007.

Jones, Wendell. "Complex Adaptive System." In Beyond Intractability, edited by Guy Burgess and Heidi Burgess. Last modified October 2003. Conflict Research Consortium, University of Colorado, Boulder, Colorado, USA. http://www.beyondintractability.org/essay/complex_adaptive_systems/

Kaldor, Mary. "Old Wars, Cold Wars, New Wars, and the War on Terror." Lecture given to the Cold War Studies Centre, London School of Economics, London, February 2005.

------. *New and Old Wars: Organized Violence in a Global Era*. 2nd ed. Palo Alto: Stanford University Press, 2007.

Kant, Immanuel. "Idea for a Universal History from a Cosmopolitan Point of View." 1784. In *On History*. Translated by Lewis White Beck. Indianapolis: Bobbs-Merrill, 1963.

Kanter, Emanuel. *The Evolution of War: A Marxian Study*. Chicago: Charles H. Kerr & Company, 1927.

Keegan, John. *A History of Warfare*. 2nd ed. London: Pimlico, 2004.

Keen, David J. *Complex Emergencies*. Cambridge: Polity Press, 2008.

Kilcullen, David. *The Accidental Guerilla: Fighting Small Wars in the Midst of a Big One*. Oxford: Oxford University Press, 2009.

Klotz, Audie, and Cecilia Lynch. "Le constructivisme dans la théorie des relations internationales." *Critique internationale* 2 (2009):51-62.

Knightley, Phillip. *The First Casualty: The War Correspondent as Hero and Myth-Maker from the Crimea to Kosovo*. Revised ed. Baltimore, MD: Johns Hopkins University Press, 2002.

Lamarche, Jacques. *La Dynastie des Lanthier*. Montréal: Pierre Tisseyre, 1973.

Langlois, Eric. "Guerre classique et guerre révolutionnaire: l'illusion de la différence." *Stratégique* 85 (May 2005).

Laue, Theodore H. von. "Reflections on War and Peace." *History and Theory* 37, no.1 (1998):111-123.

Launay, Stephen. "Quelques formes et raisons de la guerre." *Raisons politiques* 13 (2004):9-35.

Le Moigne, Jean-Louis. *La Modélisation des Systèmes Complexes*. Paris: Dunod, 1999.

Leboeuf, Anline. "Fluid Conflicts: Concepts and Scenarios." *Politique étrangère* (Septembre 2005):625–638.

Lebow, Richard Ned. *Why Nations Fight*. Cambridge: Cambridge University Press, 2010.

Lefort, Claude. "Lectures de la guerre: le Clausewitz de Raymond Aron." *Annales – Économies, Sociétés, Civilisations* 32, no.6 (1977):1268-1279.

------. *Le travail de l'oeuvre de Machiavel*. Paris: Gallimard, 1986.

Lenin, Vladimir I. "War and Revolution." 1929. In *Lenin: Collected Works*, vol.24:398-421. Moscow: Progress Publishers, 1964.

------. *Imperialism, the Highest Stage of Capitalism: A Popular Outline*. 1917. Reprint, Beijing: Foreign Languages Press, 1970.

Liang, Qiao, and Wang Xiangsui. *Unrestricted Warfare*. Beijing: PLA Literature and Arts Publishing House, 1999.

Lindemann, Thomas. "Des guerriers pour faire la paix: L'Armée américaine en Irak." *Cultures & Conflits* 67 (Fall 2007):13-34.

------. *La guerre: Théories, Causes, Règlements*. Paris: Armand Colin, 2010.

------. *Causes of War: The Struggle for Recognition*. Colchester: ECPR Press, 2010.

Lloyd, Geoffrey Ernest Richard. *Demystifying Mentalities*. Cambridge: Cambridge University Press, 2004.

Lorenz, Edward N. *The Essence of Chaos*. Seattle: University of Washington Press, 1993.

Luttwak, Edward. *Strategy: The Logic of War and Peace*. Cambridge, MA: The Belknap Press of Harvard University Press, 2001.

Machiavelli, Niccolò. "Discourses On the First Ten Books of Titus Livius." 1517. In *The Historical, Political, and Diplomatic Writings of Niccolo Machiavelli*. Translated by Christian E. Detmold. Boston: J. R. Osgood and company, 1882. http://oll.libertyfund.org/index/php?option=com_staticxt&staticfile=show.php&title=774

------. *Art of War*. 1520. Translated by Christopher Lynch. Reprint, Chicago: University of Chicago, 2003.

------. *The Prince*. 1532. Translated by Harvey C. Mansfield. Reprint, Chicago: University of Chicago , 1998.

Malesevic, Sinisa. "The Sociology of New Wars? Assessing the Causes and Objectives of Contemporary Violent Conflicts." *International Political Sociology* 2, no.2 (2008):92-112.

Marchal, Roland, and Christine Messiant. "De l'avidité des rebelles. L'analyse économique de la guerre civile selon Paul Collier." *Critique internationale* 16 (2002):58-69.

Marx, Karl. *The Eighteenth Brumaire of Louis Bonaparte*. 1852. Reprint, New York: International Publishers, 1990.

------, and Friedrich Engels. *Manifesto of the Communist Party*. 1848. Reprint, New York: Cosimo Classics, 2009.

Mayer, Bernard. *The Dynamics of Conflict Resolution*. San Francisco: Jossey-Bass, 2000.

Miller, John H., and Scott E. Page. *Complex Adaptive Systems: An Introduction to Computational Models of Social Life*. Princeton: Princeton University Press, 2007.

Mitleton-Kelly, Eve, ed. *Complex Systems and Evolutionary Perspectives of Organisations: The Application of Complexity Theory to Organisations*. Amsterdam: Pergamon, 2003.

Montesquieu, Charles de Secondat. *Pensées*. Paris: Robert Lafont, 1991.

------. *The Spirit of Laws*. 1748. Translated by Thomas Nugent. Reprint, New York: Cosimo, 2007.

Morin, Edgar. "Restricted Complexity, General Complexity." Translated by Carlos Gershenson. Paper presented at the colloquium *Intelligence de la complexité: épistémologie et pragmatique*, Cerisy-La-Salle, France, June 26, 2005. Issued from *Worldviews, Science and Us: Philosophy and Complexity*, University of Liverpool, UK, September 11-14, 2005.
http://eproceedings.worldscinet.com/9789812707420/9789812707420_0002.html

------. *Introduction à la pensée complexe*. Paris: Editions du Seuil, 2005.

------. *La complexité humaine*. Paris: Flammarion, 1994.

Moten, Matthew, ed. *Between War and Peace: How America Ends its Wars*. New York: Free Press, 2011.

Mucchielli, Roger. *La subversion*. Paris: CLC, 1976.

Münkler, Herfried. *The New Wars*. Cambridge: Polity Press, 2005.

Nederman, Cary. "Niccolò Machiavelli." In *The Stanford Encyclopedia of Philosophy*, Fall 2009 ed.. Accessed June 21, 2011.
http://plato.stanford.edu/archives/fall2009/entries/machiavelli/

Nemeth, Stephen. *Adaptive Tactics: Terrorist Targeting and Regime Type*. University of Iowa. Paper prepared for a presentation at the Midwest Political Science Association Annual Meeting, Chicago, Illinois, April 20-23, 2006. http://myweb.uiowa.edu/snemeth/mpsaterrorismpaper.pdf

Niccholls, David, and Todor Tagarev. "What Does Chaos Theory Mean for Warfare?" *Airpower Journal* (Fall 1994).

Owens, Patricia. *Between War and Politics: International Relations and the Thought of Hannah Arendt*. New York: Oxford University Press, 2007.

PA Consulting Group, *Dynamic Planning for COIN in Afghanistan*, December 2009. http://msnbcmedia.msn.com/i/MSNBC/Components/Photo/_new/Afghanistan_Dynamic_Planning.pdf

Page, Scott E. *Diversity and Complexity*. Princeton: Princeton University Press, 2011.

Perlstein, Rick. "Not in his father's footsteps." *Los Angeles Times*. February 10, 2008.

Patočka, Jan. *Heretical Essays in the Philosophy of History*. Chicago: Open Court, 1996.

Rahe, Paul A. *Montesquieu and the Logic of Liberty*. New Haven: Yale University Press, 2009.

Ramsbotham, Oliver, Tome Woodhouse, and Hugh Miall. *Contemporary Conflict Resolution*. 2nd ed. Cambridge: Polity Press, 2009.

Raufer, Xavier. *Les nouveaux dangers planétaires: Chaos mondial, décèlement précoce*. Paris: CNRS Editions, 2009.

Reno, William. "The Politics of Insurgency in Collapsing States." *Development and Change* 33, no.5 (2002):837-858.

------. *Warlord Politics and African States*. Boulder: Rienner, 1998.

Richani, Nazih. *Systems of Violence: The Political Economy of War and Peace in Colombia*. New York: State University of New York Press, 2002.

Rogers, Simon. "The McChrystal Afghanistan PowerPoint slide: can you do any better?" *The Guardian*. April 29, 2010.

Rosen, Stephen Peter. *War and Human Nature*. Princeton: Princeton University Press, 2005.

Roubelat, Fabrice. "Aide à la décision. Technique et stratégie." *Stratégique* 54, no.2 (1992).

Roy, Olivier. "Afghanistan: la guerre comme facteur de passage au politique. "*Revue française de science politique* 39, no.6 (1989):887-902.

------. "Afghanistan: les raisons d'un conflit interminable." *Cultures & Conflits* 1 (Winter 1990):13-23.

Ruggiero, Vincenzo. *Understanding Political Violence: A Criminological Analysis*. London: Open University Press, 2006.

Scales, Robert H. "Adaptive Enemies: Achieving Victory by Avoiding Defeat." *Joint Force Quarterly* 23 (Autumn/Winter 1999/2000):7-14.

Schelling, Thomas. *The Strategy of Conflict*. 1960. Reprint, Cambridge MA: Harvard University Press, 1981.

Scheper-Hughes, Nancy, and Philippe Bourgois, eds. *Violence in War and Peace: An Anthology*. Malden: Blackwell Publishing, 2004.

Schuurman, Bart. "Clausewitz and the 'New Wars' Scholars." *Parameters* (Spring 2010):89-100.

Sen, Amartya. *Identity and Violence*. London: Penguin, 2007.

Simmel, Georg. "The Sociology of Conflict I." *The American Journal of Sociology* 9, no.4 (1904):490-525.

------. "The Sociology of Conflict II." *The American Journal of Sociology* 9, no.5 (1904):672-689.

------. "The Sociology of Conflict III." *The American Journal of Sociology* 9, no.6 (1904):798-811.

Smith, Rupert. *The Utility of Force: The Art of War in The Modern World*. London: Vintage, 2008.

Sun Tzu. *The Art of War*. Translated by Samuel B. Griffith. London: Oxford University Press, 1971.

Suratteau, Jean-François. *La Politique est-elle la Guerre continuée par d'autres moyens?* Paris: Editions Archétype 82, 2010.

Taleb, Nassim Nicholas. *The Bed of Procrustes: Philosophical and Practical Aphorisms*. New York: Random House, 2010.

------. *The Black Swan: The Impact of the Highly Probable*. New York: Random House, 2007.

Teilhard de Chardin, Pierre. *Writings in Time of War*. Translated by René Hague. London: Collins, 1968.

Terray, Emmanuel. *Clausewitz*. Paris: Fayard, 1999.

Terrel, Jean. "Guerre." In *Dictionnaire électronique Montesquieu*. February 2008. http://dictionnaire-montesquieu.ens-lyon.fr/index.php?id=362

------. "Paix." In *Dictionnaire électronique Montesquieu*. February 2008. http://dictionnaire-montesquieu.ens-lyon.fr/index.php?id=363

The Wire. Season III, episode 12. DVD. Directed by David Simon. New York: HBO, 2006.

Thibault, Jean-François. "La politique comme pure acte de guerre: Clausewitz, Schmitt et Foucault." *Monde Commun* 1, no.1 (2007):114-129.

Thucydides. *The History of the Peloponnesian War*. Translated by Rex Warner. London: Penguin, 1972.

Tilly, Charles. "War Makind and State Making as Organized Crime." In *Bringing the State Back In*, edited by Peter Evans, Dietrich Rueschemeyer, and Theda Skocpol, 169-187. Cambridge: Cambridge University Press, 1985.

Trungpa, Chögyam. *Orderly Chaos: The Mandala Principle*. Boston: Shambhala, 1991.

Waltz, Kenneth N. "The Origins of War in Neorealist Theory." *Journal of Interdisciplinary History* 18, no.4 (Spring, 1988):615-628.

------. *Man, the State, and War*. 2nd Revised ed. New York: Columbia University Press, 2001.

Weeks, Michael R. "Chaos, Complexity, and Conflict." *Air & Space Power Journal* (July 2001).

Wendt, Alexander. "Anarchy is What States Make of It: The Social Construction of Power Politics." *International Organization* 46, no.2 (1992):391-425.

Woodrow Wilson International Center. *The Economics of War: The Intersection of Need, Creed and Greed*. Conference report, September 10, 2001. http://tinyurl.com/2g77tup

Congo

Beneduce, Roberto, L. Jourdan, T. Raeymaekers, and K. Vlassenroot. "Violence with a purpose: exploring the functions and meaning of violence in the Democratic Republic of Congo." *Intervention: International Journal of Mental Health, Psychosocial Work and Counseling in Areas of Armed Conflict* 4, no.1 (2006):32-46.

Clark, John F., ed. *The African Stakes of the Congo War*. New York: Palgrave Macmillan, 2002.

De Villers, Gauthier. "Identifications et mobilisations politiques au Congo-Kinshasa." *Politique Africaine* 72 (1998):81-97.

------. "La guerre dans les évolutions du Congo-Kinshasa." *Afrique Contemporaine* 215, (2005):47-70.

------. *Republique démocratique du Congo - Guerre et politique: Les trente derniers mois de L.D. Kabila (août 1998-janvier 2001)*. Paris: L'Harmattan, 2001.

------, and Jean-Claude Willame. *Republique démocratique du Congo – Chronique politique d'un entre-deux-guerres (octobre 1996-juillet 1998)*. Paris: L'Harmattan, 1998.

Doom, Ruddy, and Jan Gorus, eds. *Politics of Identity and Economics of Conflict in the Great Lakes Region*. Brussels: VUB University Press, 2000.

Insight on Conflict. *DRCongo*. Online report. Accessed June 21, 2011. http://www.insightonconflict.org/conflicts/dr-congo/

Jourdan, Luca. "Being at War, Being Young: Violence and Youth in North Kivu." In *Conflict and Social Transformation in Eastern DR Congo*, edited by Koen Vlassenroot and Timothy Raeymaekers, 157-175. Ghent: Academia Press, 2004.

La Documentation Française. *Le conflit des grands lacs en Afrique*. Online report. Last modified February 2007. http://www.ladocumentationfrancaise.fr/dossiers/conflit-grands-lacs/index.shtml

Mathieu, Paul, and Jean-Claude Willame, eds. *Conflicts et Guerres au Kivu et dans la région des Grands Lacs: Entre tensions locales et escalade régionale*. Paris: L'Harmattan, 1999.

Mbavu Muhindo, Vincent. *Le Congo-Zaïre d'une guerre à l'autre: de Libération en Occupation.* Paris: L'Harmattan, 2003.

Pourtier, Roland. "Le Kivu dans la guerre: acteurs et enjeux." *EchoGéo* (January 2009). http://echogeo.revues.org/10793

Raeymaekers, Timothy. "Sharing the Spoils: The Reinvigoration of Congo's Political System." *Politorbis* 42, no.1 (2007):23-29.

------. *Collapse or Order? Questionning State Collapse in Africa.* Working paper, Conflict Research Group – University of Ghent (May 2005).

------. *Network War: An Introduction to Congo's Privatized War Economy.* IPIS Report (October 2002).

Reyntjens, Filip. "Briefing: The Second Congo War: More Than a Remake." *African Affairs* 98, no.391 (1999):241-250.

------. *La Guerre des Grands Lacs: Alliances mouvantes et conflits extraterritoriaux en Afrique centrale.* Paris: L'Harmattan, 1999.

------. *The Great African War: Congo and Regional Geopolitics, 1996–2006.* New York: Cambridge University Press, 2009.

------, and Stefaan Marysse, eds. *L'Afrique des Grands Lacs: Dix ans de transitions conflictuelles – Annuaire 2005/2006.* Paris: L'Harmattan, 2006.

Solvit, Samuel. *Clausewitz and Modern Wars: Is Clausewitz's Political Conception of War Still Pertinent, and Is It Applicable to New Realities?* The American University of Paris. May 2010.

------. *RDC: Rêve ou illusion? Conflits et ressources naturelles en République démocratique du Congo.* Paris: L'Harmattan, 2009.

Turner, Thomas. *The Congo Wars: Conflict, Myth, and Reality.* London: Zed, 2008.

United Nations. *Final Report of the Panel of Experts on the Illegal Exploitation of Natural Resources and Other Forms of Wealth of the Democratic Republic of the Congo.* S/2002/1146, October 2002.

Vedby, Rasmussen Mikkel. *The Risk Society at War: Terror, Technology and Strategy in the Twenty-first Century.* Cambridge: Cambridge University Press, 2006.

Vlassenroot, Koen, and Timothy Raeymaekers. "The Politics of Rebellion and Intervention in Ituri: The Emergence of a New Political Complex?" *African Affairs* 103, no.412 (2004):385-412.

------. *The Formation New Political Complexes: Dynamics of Conflict in Ituri*, Working paper, Centre of African Studies – University of Copenhagen (October 2003).

------. *The Formation of Centres of Profit, Power, and Protection: Conflict and Social Transformation in Eastern DR Congo.* Working paper, Centre of African Studies – University of Copenhagen, (January 2005).

------, and Timothy Raeymaekers, eds. *Conflict and Social Transformation in Eastern DR Congo.* Ghent: Academia Press, 2004.

Weiss, Herbert. "War and Peace in the Democratic Republic of the Congo." *Current African Issues*, Nordiska Afrikainstitutet, no.22 (2000):1-29.

Willame, Jean-Claude. *La Guerre du Kivu: Vues de la salle climatisée et de la véranda.* Brussels: Editions GRIP, 2010.

Williams, Michael J. *NATO, Security and Risk Management: from Kosovo to Kandahar.* London: Routledge, 2009.

Vietnam

Caputo, Philip. *10,000 Days of Thunder: A History of the Vietnam War*. New York: Atheneum, 2005.

Cerami, Joseph R. "Presidential Decisionmaking and Vietnam: Lessons for Strategists." *Parameters* 26 (Winter 1996–97):66-80.

Colby, William. *Lost Victory: A Firsthand Account of America's Sixteen-Year Involvement in Vietnam*. Chicago: Contemporary Books, 1989.

Gelb, Leslie H., and Richard K. Betts. *The Irony of Vietnam: the System Worked*. Washington: The Brookings Institution, 1979.

Haugen, David, and Susan Musser, eds. *Perspectives on Modern World History: The Vietnam War*. Farmington Hills: Greenhaven Press, 2011.

Herring, George C. "America and Vietnam: The Unending War." *Foreign Affairs* 70, no.5 (Winter 1991):104-119.

------. *America's Longest War: The United States and Vietnam, 1950–1975*. 4th ed. New York: McGraw-Hill, 2002.

Karnow, Stanley. *Vietnam: A History*. 2nd ed. New York: Penguin, 1997.

Kissinger, Henry. *Diplomacy*. New York: Touchstone, 1994.

Lind, Michael. *Vietnam, the Necessary War: A Reinterpretation of America's Most Disastrous Military Conflict*. New York: The Free Press, 1999.

Logevall, Fredrik. *Choosing War: The Lost Chance for Peace and the Escalation of War in Vietnam*. Berkeley: University of California Press, 2001.

Mandelbaum, Michael. "Vietnam: The Television War." *Daedalus* 111, no.4 (Fall 1982):157-169.

McNamara, Robert S., James G. Blight, and Robert K Brigham. *Argument Without End: In Search of Answers to the Vietnam Tragedy*, New York: Public Affairs, 1999.

Nitzschke, Stephen G. *Vietnam: A Complex Adaptive Perspective*. United States Marine Corps (1997). http://smallwarsjournal.com/documents/nitzschke.pdf

Olson, Gregory Allen. *Landmark Speeches on the Vietnam War*. College Station: Texas A&M University Press, 2010.

Perlstein, Rick. "Not in his father's footsteps," *Los Angeles Times*, February 10, 2008.

Rose, Gideon. *How Wars End – Why We Always Fight the Last Battle*. New York: Simon & Schuster, 2010.

Rougé, Jean-Robert, ed. *L'opinion américaine de la guerre du Vietnam*. Paris: Presses de l'Université de Paris-Sorbonne, 1992.

Shane-Armstrong, Ryn. *The Vietnam War: Great Speeches in History*. Farmington Hills: Greenhaven, 2002.

Small, Melvin. *At the Water's Edge: American Politics and the Vietnam War*. Lanham: Ivan R Dee, 2006.

Smith, Ralph B. *An International History of the Vietnam War. Volume II: The Struggle for South-East Asia 1961-65*. Houndmills: Macmillan Press, 1985.

ABBREVIATIONS

CAS	Complex Adaptive System
DRC	Democratic Republic of the Congo
NATO	North Atlantic Treaty Organization
RCD	Rally for Congolese Democracy
UN	United Nations
UNITA	National Union for Total Independence of Angola
US	United States of America

L'HARMATTAN, ITALIA
Via Degli Artisti 15; 10124 Torino

L'HARMATTAN HONGRIE
Könyvesbolt ; Kossuth L. u. 14-16
1053 Budapest

ESPACE L'HARMATTAN KINSHASA
Faculté des Sciences sociales,
politiques et administratives
BP243, KIN XI
Université de Kinshasa

L'HARMATTAN CONGO
67, av. E. P. Lumumba
Bât. – Congo Pharmacie (Bib. Nat.)
BP2874 Brazzaville
harmattan.congo@yahoo.fr

L'HARMATTAN GUINÉE
Almamya Rue KA 028, en face du restaurant Le Cèdre
OKB agency BP 3470 Conakry
(00224) 60 20 85 08
harmattanguinee@yahoo.fr

L'HARMATTAN CAMEROUN
BP 11486
Face à la SNI, immeuble Don Bosco
Yaoundé
(00237) 99 76 61 66
harmattancam@yahoo.fr

L'HARMATTAN CÔTE D'IVOIRE
Résidence Karl / cité des arts
Abidjan-Cocody 03 BP 1588 Abidjan 03
(00225) 05 77 87 31
etien_nda@yahoo.fr

L'HARMATTAN MAURITANIE
Espace El Kettab du livre francophone
N° 472 avenue du Palais des Congrès
BP 316 Nouakchott
(00222) 63 25 980

L'HARMATTAN SÉNÉGAL
« Villa Rose », rue de Diourbel X G, Point E
BP 45034 Dakar FANN
(00221) 33 825 98 58 / 77 242 25 08
senharmattan@gmail.com

L'HARMATTAN TOGO
1771, Bd du 13 janvier
BP 414 Lomé
Tél : 00 228 2201792
gerry@taama.net

544099 - Octobre 2013
Achevé d'imprimer par

Made in the USA
Monee, IL
03 May 2026